Light in the Darkness

Paul Banthorpe

Kingdom Publishers

Light in the Darkness
Copyright© Paul Banthorpe

All rights reserved. No part of this book may be reproduced in any form by photocopying or any electronic or mechanical means, including information storage or retrieval systems, without permission in writing from both the copyright owner and the publisher of the book. The right of Paul Banthorpe to be identified as the author of this work has been asserted by him in accordance with the Copyright, Designs and Patents Act 1988 and any subsequent amendments thereto. A catalogue record for this book is available from the British Library.

All Scripture Quotations have been taken from the New International Version of the Bible.

ISBN: 978-1-913247-90-4

1st Edition by Kingdom Publishers

Kingdom Publishers
London, UK.

You can purchase copies of this book from any leading bookstore or email **contact@kingdompublishers.co.uk**

Dedication

This book is dedicated to all those who have lost loved ones due to Covid-19. The light shines in the darkness, and the darkness has not overcome it

Content

Foreword	11
Prologue	13
March 2020	17
21st March: *Islands*	17
22nd March: *The Greenhouse*	19
23rd March: *Lockdown*	21
24th March: *Operation Extraction*	23
25th March: *Mind Games*	25
26th March: *Clap for Carers*	27
27th March: *Police State*	29
28th March: *A Stark Choice*	31
29th March: *Adaptation*	33
30th March: *Stranded*	35
31st March: *Origins*	37
APRIL 2020	38
1st April: *Slow Motion*	38
4th April : *Vital signs*	40
5th April: *Queen of Hearts*	42
7th April: *Resilience*	44
8th April: *Rainbows*	46
10th April: *Lottie*	48
12th April: *The Portabella Priest*	50
14th April: *A Dogs Life*	52

15th April: *99 Not Out*	*54*
17th April: *Space Oddity*	*56*
18th April: *Cabin Fever*	*58*
19th April: *Bread and Wine*	*60*
20th April: *A Bit of a Mess*	*62*
22nd April: *Satellites*	*64*
23rd April: *Am I Bovverred?*	*66*
25th April: *Milestones*	*69*
26th April: *In Denial*	*71*
27th April: *The New Normal*	*73*
29th April: *Birthday Wishes*	*75*
30th April: *Living by Numbers*	*77*

MAY 2020

1st May: *Back in the USSR*	*80*
3rd May: *Expectant Prayer*	*83*
4th May: *(Be with You)*	*85*
6th May: *Cat's Eyes*	*86*
7th May: *You'll Never Walk Alone*	*88*
8th May: *VE Day*	*91*
10th May: *The Big Exit Plan*	*94*
12th May: *Lady of the Lamp*	*97*
14th May: *Fairies and Imps*	*99*
15th May: *Exposing the Divide*	*101*
16th May: *To Bee or Not to Bee*	*104*
17th May: *Virtual Reality*	*106*
18th May: *Kindness*	*109*
20th May: *Zoom – Unknown Territory*	*111*
21st May: *Taking the Shackles off*	*114*
22nd May: *Class of '36*	*117*
24th May: *Jigsaws*	*120*
25th May: *Trial and No Error*	*122*
27th May: *Can't Live Without…..*	*125*
28th May: *Test and Trace*	*128*
29th May: *The Dark Web*	*130*

30th May: *Reinventing the Wheel* — 133
31st May: *Explanation Ready* — 136

JUNE 2020

1st June: *Manic Monday* — 151
2nd June: *It Must Be Love!* — 153
4th June: *The Perfect Storm (Part 1)* — 155
5th June: *The Perfect Storm (Part 2)* — 158
6th June: *Behind the Mask* — 161
7th June: *40* — 163
8th June: *Quarantine* — 165
10th June: *Rhythm and Blues* — 167
11th June: *Statues* — 169
13th June: *I'm Forever Blowing Bubbles* — 171
13th June: *Love is a Battlefield* — 174
14th June: *On Mission* — 177
15th June: *Retail Therapy* — 180
17th June: *Food for Thought* — 182
19th June: *Muppet Mayhem* — 184
20th June: *Such a Big Girl!* — 187
21st June: *God The Father* — 189
23rd June: *Bird's Eye View* — 192
24th June: *A Stitch in Time* — 195
26th June: *30 Years of Hurt* — 198
27th June: *On a Knife Edge* — 200
29th June: *Patient 91* — 202
30th June: *Schools of Thought* — 205

JULY 2020

1st July: *Divided Loyalties* — 208
3rd July: *Unchained Melody* — 212
4th July: *Inn Dependence Day* — 215
5th July: *Audacious Hope* — 217
7th July: *Sticky Situation* — 220

9th July: *The Sound of Music*	223
11th July: *Identity*	226
12th July: *Shaken and …Stirred*	231
14th July: *Painting by Numbers*	232
15th July: *Praise Sandwich*	234
16th July: *Cyber Wars*	237
17th July: *Longevity*	239
18th July: *Prayer for the World*	241
19th July: *On the Frontline*	244
20th July: *Pecking Order*	247
22nd July: *From Russia without Love*	250
24th July: *The Great British Cover Up*	253
26th July: *Bread*	256
26th July: *Leava La Espana*	259
28th July: *Duty of Care*	261
30th July: *Going Back in the Water*	264
31st July: *Inheritance*	267
1st August: *The Lighthouse*	270
Epilogue	274

Foreword

March 2020 was the month when everything changed, the nation plunged into the world of covid crises lockdown as we collectively responded to the invisible pandemic threat to our freedoms and ways of living. However, despite the fear and agitation, it was also a time of reflection and wonder. I remember the eery quiet streets in the early evenings, bike rides and runs with nobody in sight. The sound of bird song replacing the roar of usual background traffic and skies free of aeroplanes as foreign travel was put on hold.

Paul beautifully captures this balance of worry and wonder in a beautiful way as he frames the first lockdown lessons learned in his own home against the growing national portrait. It is heart-warming and real as the challenge of the family learning to work from home evolves into idiosyncratic irritations, often overcome by grace, tolerance and acceptance. The pain of separation from loved ones and the strain of screen-based interactions is never overplayed but simply portrayed with a keen heartfelt honesty

The real strength of Light in the Darkness is that Paul manages to artfully avoid self-indulgent reflection with humility and a wry turn of phrase. Light in the Darkness covers an international crisis from the sofa of the writer's living room where Jess the Cockerpoo and Lottie the one-eyed tabby cat hold court.

Faith based reflections nestle against familiar news reports that serve as way markers, leading us through the lockdown. The bravery of Captain

Tom Moore and the heartfelt exuberance of the Thursday evening NHS clap are just two of many stories noted.

Light in the Darkness made me roar with laughter as I recognise so much of myself in Paul's stories. Reading the narrative also made me wince when I recall like Paul, the number of aimless hours spent watching TV on the sofa. Yet throughout Paul demonstrates how to hold on to faith in a crisis and brings Bible passages alive, connecting them to real life domestic situations.

Light in the Darkness is hard to truly categorise as it is in parts, a personal journal, a social commentary and a biblical devotional. It will appeal to both people of no faith and people of great faith and anyone in between.

This could easily be serialised as a podcast or as a series of magazine columns – I certainly hope Paul continues to write in this way. I look forward to Pauls observations on the post pandemic landscape. An idea for a sequel perhaps?

Rev Graham McBain

Prologue

March 2020. We had just entered what we know now as the *first* national lockdown in England. The case numbers and recorded deaths in Italy from this new coronavirus strain were ringing alarm bells in London. It was time for the UK Government to take its opening gambit in what was to become an ever increasingly complex game of *life-chess*. The rules of this game were largely unknown, and in the months to follow a battle on personal, family, community, national and global fronts would unfold, the like not experienced in generations. The like we may hopefully never experience again.

I sat down in my small office bedroom space, a week after all the schools and colleges in England had closed their doors to all but the most vulnerable. I read and re-read the day's headlines in between work emails and Googled research on how best to use Microsoft Teams for teaching and learning. My attention though was drawn towards the use of online communication as a means of real time engagement with the outside world. *Education UK* has been slow to adapt to the social networking world of Snapchat, Twitter, Instagram, and to the digital age in general. Yet, what better way to meet the learning styles of our post Millennial students? Why have we taken so long to transform our classrooms; from the traditional teacher led learning space established in post War Britain, to an environment where pedagogy and technology merge in perfect synergy to become the norm in our schools, colleges and Universities? No doubt, the answer from change protagonists would include reference to *public funding short-sightedness, education suffering from being the political football of the C20th and a lack of political vision.* From opponents of change: *where does the teaching of Shakespeare fit into this anarchic e-learning revolution?*

In my current role as Head of Teaching and Learning at a Further Education college just five minutes' drive from the family home, I felt duty bound to change hearts and minds, and use this period of quieter reflection at home to advance the cause of progress. I also knew such a fundamental shift in the way we educate our young people would not happen overnight, even with the sudden imposition of remote learning as a result of a global pandemic. Rome was not built in a day of course, and as we would be constantly reminded over the next six months, a vaccine for Covid-19 would not suddenly appear over the horizon like a syringe on horseback charging towards victory.

In the early days of forced confinement in our homes, there was a sense of surreal bewilderment. With daily national death rates in the teens and the pandemic perceived as a 'somebody else's' issue, the mood was one of accepted inconvenience rather than blind panic. The government's daily briefings had already become compulsive viewing and their associated messages were imprinted into our subconscious. *We have a plan*, Boris trumpeted in the briefing on 20th March, and *if we all stick to that plan*, we would beat this pandemic, sending it back into oblivion with its tail between its legs. A national three-month lockdown they assured us would achieve this victory. Boris was in charge standing on the central dais flanked by two trusty Lieutenants; Whitty and Sunak. The Commander in Chief was in full Churchillian mode.

'So that's why, as far as possible, we want you to stay at home, that's how we can protect our NHS and save lives.

To repeat, I know how difficult this is, how it seems to go against the freedom-loving instincts of the British people. And I also know how much, right now, workers and business deserve the financial reassurance we are giving them.

But we will get through this.

We will get through it together, and we will beat this virus.

And to ram that point home: the more effectively we follow the advice that we are given, the faster this country will stage both a medical and an economic recovery in full'.

I was waiting for the....*never in the field of human conflict*...

I collected my thoughts that evening as we sat in the living room and considered how this lockdown would affect our own family dynamics. My wife Diana also works in education as a part-time learning support assistant at another nearby college. Her stay at home brief was to provide online help for students on a one-to-one basis. Diana has two children from her first marriage, Daniel who is a radio presenter and Sarah who is studying a Psychology degree at Reading University. Just to confuse the outside world, I too have a son from my first marriage who lives with us, also called Daniel. So, to distinguish between the two boys, we have 22-year-old 'Big Dan' and 16-year-old *'Little Dan'* or just *Daniel* when he shows an ounce of maturity.

Unable to access studios in London's Golden Square Big Dan set up a make-shift audio arrangement in his bedroom to record several shows every week. Little Dan meanwhile would be sent GCSE work to him on a daily basis by his teachers. His response was to set up an enhanced gaming desk in his bedroom so he could get the most of lockdown. Sarah was still in Reading much to her mum's distress, holed up in a student house near the University. As we entered this period of constrained movement, we knew our pets would begin to sense a change in their environment. Lottie the ageing tabby, Mo the middle-aged Maine Coon, and Jess the puppy Cockerpoo would play their part in either keeping us calm or driving us into insanity. It was a toss of a coin.

Fortunately, we are blessed to live in a large house tucked away in a secluded crescent halfway between the Surrey towns of Redhill and Reigate. I want to make this clear from the start; what you are about to read is not a story of hardship or tragedy. It is not a great tale of redemption or salvation. It was initially just an attempt at writing a daily blog during the first lockdown to see if I could enter this brave new world of social networking. In doing so, this middle aged technophobe could start to understand 'the kids' and connect with their inner hashtag.

Perhaps it could be the cathartic experience I needed to help maintain a sense of perspective, as I sat in my comfortable suburban home with my post postmodern nuclear family unit. Maybe it would help to relieve some of the guilt when reading about others who were about to deal with Covid-19 head on. Maybe I wanted to use the blog as a distraction from the new mundane, or as a reflective mirror of words and observations as the headlines came pouring through the airwaves. So, the day after Boris' above briefing, I started typing on a wing and a prayer. Maybe it would last one week, maybe two at best before I grew tired of my own whimsy.

I was wrong. By the third week of writing it no longer felt like a simple blog to self. Each entry became part of a growing sense of conviction; with one question nagging at me with every sentence written. *Where is God's plan in Covid-19?*

As a Christian the dilemma in knowing a God of love but seeing the suffering of a groaning world is the hardest part of the big faith equation. I try not to beat myself up about it. Can such a question ever be fully reconciled in the human mind? I do not pretend for one moment that writing 100 blog entries during the first Covid lockdown begins to touch the depth of such a question. However, I also make no apology for sharing my beliefs in a God I have known for thirty years. A God who has kept faithful with me, even when I have turned the other way. A God who despite my human failings has often revealed a plan not just for my life, but for those friends and family around me who share the same conviction.

What I did not expect was how God would take me in new directions, pointing me to passages of scripture I did not know, and leading me on a journey of hope as I wrestled with my own doubts. As I gradually opened up my Blog to others (never an original intention), it was *His* words which gave meaning to my imperfect ramblings. Like a road map slowly unfolding to show the path ahead, the God of all creation peered into the darkness called Covid-19 and breathed light into its midst. This divine intervention gave me the sense of perspective I was looking for, but also left me with a set of clues from which to respond. The ending of my personal blog journey was as unexpected as it was remarkable. I hope and pray your journey will also be touched by the illuminating word of God, and a plan for your life revealed, just as promised in the book of Jeremiah.

'For I know the plans I have for you,' declares the LORD, 'plans to prosper you and not to harm you, plans to give you hope and a future'.

March 2020

21st March: *Islands*

'No man is an island' wrote John Bonne in his famous poem of 1624. It is hard to argue with this sentiment for we all need someone. We are created to be social creatures who thrive on human interaction. But as of today, we have been told to go against this natural instinct, for our own sake, and for the sake of those around us. We have been told to be 'islands'.

After what seems like an age of grey dreariness, a bright Spring sky watches over England's fair and pleasant land. The new dreariness to contend with is a world of social distancing and self-isolation. This instructed shift in behaviour is going to take commitment, self-discipline and sacrifice. And a great deal of practice.

At 9 O'clock this morning five adults and four dogs from our road spent an hour trampling through local wooded paths, often walking in near proximity to each other. Tangled leads, close harmonised gossip, and frequent side-steps to avoid on-coming human traffic, were a regular feature of the walk. *Quite frankly*, we struggled to be 'islands'. Yet, we were not alone. In Australia, Bondi Beach closed to stop crowds from pleasuring themselves in the warm surf. In the United States, police were called upon to break up large gatherings of youths in several major cities.

By this afternoon vast throngs were out enjoying the early Spring sunshine in our own coastal resorts and national parks. In fact, Snowdonia reported record numbers of visitors cascading through the Welsh iconic landscape. Not so much a case of 'not in my back yard', but rather, 'it surely cannot happen to me, and not here'. *The young think they are invincible*, Nicola had stated boldly on the dog walk. *They could all be carriers you know,* she added, picking up Tilly's poo.

Earlier today the world lost legendary Country singer Kenny Rogers aged 81. Rogers was probably best known for his number one duet with Dolly Parton 'Islands in the Stream' recorded in 1983. Perhaps the opening lines of the chorus describe what we are all about to experience in 2020. We are being asked to be 'islands', and for the time being, *'that is what we are'*. Yet at the same time we are ironically more reliant on each other than ever before in peacetime memory. For the foreseeable future we are all in this together, floating down the same stream of life. Separated, but intrinsically linked together in battle against an unseen deadly foe.

22nd March: *The Greenhouse*

For her birthday at the beginning of March I bought Diana a 6mx4m polycarbonate sheeting greenhouse. In hindsight this purchase looks a real winner, for now with so much time to kill, her green fingers can potter away merrily and take her mind off the current crises. However, due to an administrative mix up the huge cardboard box that contained the 'easy to erect' item had been delivered just two days ago. As today is Mother's Day her son Dan and my son Daniel offered to help build the greenhouse, while I entertained Jessica the Cockerpoo.

Well that was the initial intention. Another crystal blue sky meant another long morning dog walk. The apricot-coloured puppy could not believe her luck when mummy, daddy and the two boys took her out into the woods. The same dilemma remained when meeting other people – to greet or not greet? – that is the question. We nodded courteously, and muffled attempts of 'morning' and 'lovely day' could be heard at a safe distance. Jessica however, blatantly ignored government advice and chased everything that moved, causing her personal human entourage to engage in a constant battle to stay on the right side of the two-meter social distancing guidelines. Nerves soon frayed.

On return from our wooded ordeal the boys grabbed Magnums from the freezer and slunk off to their bedrooms for a few hours solitude. 22-year-old Dan on Playstation, 16-year-old Daniel on Xbox. Diana resigned herself to the pile of clothes washing that adorned the kitchen table, while I located the piece of lamb we had tracked down yesterday at the local butchers. *Last bit of roasting meat left in the cooler*; the butcher told us. *That's fine* replied the wife without glancing up, *we'll take it*. £22 for a joint seemed excessive, but it *was* the whole lamb with just the legs and head chopped off. This is a pandemic I reasoned with myself, and who knows when the next farm animal will become available for consumption.

Needless to say, Jamie Oliver came to rescue, and the outcome of my endeavours was four clean plates by 4 pm. After which, the sons returned to their virtual reality, the wife sat in the late afternoon glow, and the Cockerpoo had her usual mad half hour chasing Mo the cat into oblivion, before crashing out in her cage for the night.

The huge cardboard box remained unopened on the patio, its contents to be tackled another day. I thought we'd have many days to contemplate its grand opening. The UK death toll had reached 281, including an 18-year-old with an *underlying health condition*. A caveat tagline that had already become far too overfamiliar for liking.

Sitting in the lounge that evening I heard my 16-year-old son laugh in the comfort of the snug as more aliens were blasted into a thousand pixels. In the real world, an alien virus was starting to cause far more damage than that.

23rd March: *Lockdown*

First day of working – remote style. At 9.30 am, I found a corner of my absent stepdaughter's bedroom, a small desk under her Velux window providing a suitable resting place for my work laptop. I pressed the on-button and it sprung into life. The first Office Teams meeting brought me together with the other three members of the college Quality Department. This was initially just to check we were all up to internet speed and able to experience clear connectivity. After ironing out the pixel gremlins and the background rice crispy crackling, we quickly concluded that this new normal was already feeling surreal.

Further meetings came and went. Big questions were asked. Did we know if students were engaging in learning at home? Not really. Were we confident teaching staff were able to accurately measure the impact of our quick-fix on-line resources? Not really. Did we know how many vulnerable students had come into the college itself? Yes – *one*! The Level 2 Business student with moderate learning difficulties had hoped his mates would also be there too. Instead, he found himself in another form of self-isolation for the day. Several staff who had been assigned to support this directed provision could now be released to go home. It seemed for our 16-19 students, there was less appetite to 'come in' than thought. Who could blame them?

As the Head of Teaching and Learning I tried to provide some light relief and positive thinking on another MS Teams site – *share your ideas for keeping busy and working through the challenges of home working*, I posted. *Be positive everyone, we are in this together,* I wrote after putting up a link to some free digital skills training. *Look after your well-being and find new routines and interests* I posted, like some on-line oracle. There was muted response from colleagues. It's always the thought that counts I consoled myself.

Whilst struggling to find the right tune on my keyboard, Diana was enjoying the garden in the seemingly constant sun, trying to breathe new life into her mini allotment. My son washed a car for the first time in his life. My stepson set up gym equipment on the patio and sweated out his frustration at not being able to see his girlfriend who lives 30 miles away. The Cockerpoo, too young to know when to stop, played ball with everyone for hours and crashed into a semi-coma on her favourite mat. Then with cheese and biscuits on our laps, Boris came onto our screens at 8.30 looking like he had been in the wrestling ring with a COBRA. Hair coiffed in its usual hap-hazard style, he delivered another Churchillianesque speech. He praised those who had been responsible citizens and stayed at home as instructed. Then with genuine anger and frustration in his voice he reprimanded those that had not. The headmaster has spoken. Plan A was not working as well as hoped. Thousands of Brits had been sent to the naughty step.

For good reason perhaps, as infection and death rates in the UK continued to climb. Stricter social restraint measures were needed to curb the tide. We were now about to enter a full lockdown scenario.

24th March: *Operation Extraction*

Our home sits conveniently near Junction 8 of the M25. Within minutes, the grey Hyundai i20 was racing around London's orbital like a bullet train. It was an open freeway, not another car in sight. Diana sat nervously beside me, knowing we were risking the wrath of the authorities. Sweat poured down my face as the speedometer hit eighty. In forty-five minutes or so we would be at our destination, and nothing could stop us from reaching our goal.

Suddenly from nowhere a black helicopter swooped in front of the car, causing me to take evasive action. Foot down I pulled away from the aircraft as it prepared to circle. *It's alright darling*, turning to my petrified spouse with steely look in eye, *I have this under control*. Special training, past life, and all that. My right eyebrow arched higher in eager anticipation. A loud hailer boomed in our ears; *pull over slowly, you are violating the national lockdown....pull over or we will be forced to shoot.* I was doing no such thing. My stepdaughter's safety depended on it. Then from behind, two fast approaching police cars, sirens piercing as they drew up close. In the rear mirror I could see the driver of one of the black sedans. *It was Boris!* Eyes glaring behind the wheel, he looked as angry as he did the night before. The helicopter had now cut off our escape up ahead and Boris' vehicle was almost adjacent to the Hyundai. He wound down his driver window and pointed a pistol at my head. Without warning, he fired. BANG!

I sat up from the bedroom floor, sweat beads on my forehead. My right elbow hurt from the impact with the ground. I had fallen out of bed. Well, thank the Lord for that. It was just a lockdown nightmare.

The actual journey to pick up my stepdaughter from her student house in Reading, Berkshire, and return home took just over two hours. The traffic was of course much lighter than usual, mainly made up of lorries and white vans with a smattering of cars; which did make the M25 seem eerily quiet for a weekday morning. The poor girl was the last to leave her rented abode due to self-imposed isolation. Nothing but a cold and slight cough, but a wise decision in light of the current context. The announcement last night from Boris had spurred us into quick action. *"Let's get Sarah back as soon as possible"*. Diana naturally was relieved to have her daughter back in the safe haven of the family home by lunchtime.

I tried to switch back to work mode. I pressed a few buttons. Another Microsoft Teams meeting to contribute to. But as the news of fatalities at home and abroad worsened, everything else was starting to pale into insignificance. What were we planning for? The current academic year was in many respects a right off, and we were just scratching around in the dark looking for purpose and direction. As teachers and managers in schools and colleges we had to keep going, adapting approaches to teaching and learning on a daily basis; hoping for clear guidance from a government who were also wading through treacle in wellington boots. This was all unprecedented.

Today, the UK death toll rose by another 87. In Spain it was 514. In New York, the Governor pleaded for medical supplies, warning the virus was spreading faster than a bullet train. I wanted to be back in my Hyundai again, on the open road speeding to freedom. But this sadly was not a dream.

25th March: *Mind Games*

It is only five days in from the school-work shut down for millions of us plucky Brits, but the strain on the brain is already starting to tell. The first big social dilemma for us was on the 22nd March - *Mother's Day*. This caused great consternation as families were torn between visiting loved ones and respecting the social distancing rules. The young, we have been told, should not mingle with the *old* (the definition of which has also become quite a bone of contention). Many 'went for it' with fingers crossed, others used screens to bring the generations together. Since last Sunday we have moved to full lockdown. Was that intentional timing by the powers that be? Was it to allow us one more chance on Mother's Day to see family we may not see again for several months? Diana's parents are no longer with us. Mine are in self isolation mode. My mother still undergoing immunotherapy treatment, the old man 11 years her senior at 86, catching shingles completely out of the blue. At the time of writing, the technical complexities of face-to-face on-screen communication such as WhatsApp and Zoom had beaten them into early submission.

In the confusion and hubbub, Diana and I had completely forgot it was our two-year anniversary yesterday. It was as though these datelines no longer mattered. Not erased from memory of course, just eclipsed from calendar view. It is my sister's birthday today too - a key worker supporting young people with severe brain injuries. Normally we would get together for a meal, or a few cheeky shandies down the Dog and Lettuce. Not this year. Her birthday has been reduced to an e-card and a 'how's it going at your family refuge?' text.

This morning a teacher colleague of mine who lives alone in a small London flat e-mailed to say he was struggling with work for 'personal reasons'. I could read between the lines - it was an early cry for support, as I knew isolation for this flamboyant character was far from a natural state of being. On social media, messages held the same tone of despair. Sexist jokes about husbands wanting 'out' of their family lockdown nightmare, and wives and mothers losing the plot as they ran out of loo roll were rife. In my own household, only the Cockerpoo was loving life, surrounded by five humans to give her constant attention. In true adolescent droll, my teenage son declared at this early stage of lockdown; *its sound dad, I'll be fine. I've been practising self-isolation for the last two years!* He wasn't wrong.

Added to all this was the constant flow of fake news. In the last five days my eclectic family group had informed me the virus was caused by the Chinese eating bats; that it was in fact the result of an American biological weapons programme gone wrong; and that eating vast amounts of raw garlic will ward off the threat of infection. Then the wife came out with a real snorter this afternoon; Prince Charles, the heir to the British throne, had got coronavirus. LOL, not falling for that one.

On early reflection, I am personally coping pretty well as it happens. A slight worry though, as we are down to our last 27 toilet rolls.

26th March: *Clap for Carers*

At 8 O'clock tonight tens of thousands of people came out of their homes and clapped for those working on the NHS frontline. It is not an overstatement to say these public sector workers are putting themselves at considerable risk in doing their jobs. Videos of patients in hospital in the UK and abroad have brought the reality of this horror show into our living rooms. Testimonies of those who had contracted the virus and were on the road to recovery have given Covid-19 a human face. The message on the lips of TV presenters, analysts and politicians is now a national slogan; simply put - *'we are all in this together'*.

Maybe I am bias because I love my country and most of what it stands for. Maybe it is just a romantic notion, a sense of patriotism that comes through in times of crises. But is there another country in the world that has such a strong sacrificial voluntary sector? For today the call to arms has been well and truly answered again. 660,000 people have signed up to support the NHS and care services in the struggle. A miraculous number - an army of volunteers to back up an already stretched and exhausted army of healthcare professionals.

Furthermore, a blend of creativity and technology is now bringing us a stream of on-line support to the millions in walled isolation. Good news for parents attempting to home school or entertain young children, and for those on their own needing a little light in the encroaching darkness. The at-home yoga class, the innovative google based pub quiz, the live storytelling of books written by the rich and famous, and the hundreds of companies opening up delivery services for the elderly and vulnerable. Irrespective of your political persuasion, Boris deserves a pat on the back for delivering a huge financial package to keep businesses and their employers afloat. As well as finding a solution for homeowners, tenants, and the millions of self-employed who have suddenly found their earnings fall off the precipice. For many the government's work furlough scheme, a planned three month stay of execution, may be the difference between hope and despair. Its very existence tells us we are in this for the long haul.

Experts are warning us we are two weeks behind Italy - a country with a similar sophisticated and modern health care system that has been brought to its knees by the pandemic. Over 4,000 Italians have now died. In Spain, the situation is nearly as dire. Here in the UK we brace ourselves for the onslaught. On the battlefront our beloved NHS holds its breath. In support, over half a million volunteers wait in the wings. Today we applauded the great British spirit. In the months ahead we will need every ounce of that spirit to get through this...*together.*

27th March: *Police State*

Three days ago, a hundred pieces of fixtures and fittings came out the cardboard box. As I continue working remotely, now on a makeshift desk in the main bedroom, I overlook the garden area where Diana, her son, and sporadically my son, attempt to construct the greenhouse. The constant groans and swearing under the breath told me all I needed to know. The result of their efforts today? A roofless box of aluminium struts separated by lop-sided polycarbonate plastic sheets. To be fair, having glanced at the 'universally accessible diagrams' in the instruction booklet, it was surprising they had got that far. The real damage though was to the Diana's back. The stretching, twisting and regular bending to find dropped nuts and screws in the grass had taken its toll.

So, this morning, the dog routine had to be changed. As usual I was the first up to let Jess out of her sleeping crate, straight in the garden for early 'doings', and a quick breakfast for us both. A bowl of Forthglade tray chicken and liver, with biscuits on the side washed down with fresh tap water. The dog had Special K, milk and a warming mug of tea. But instead of 'mummy walkies', this morning it was 'daddy walkies' - once round the 'block' which takes about 10 minutes. Having done this walk on many occasions since we bought Jess eight months earlier, the first thing that struck me at 8 O'clock today was the silence. Not another person or car in view. There was still the low distant rumbling of traffic on the M25, but the only other noise came from a squawking murder of crows overhead, circling ominously as if waiting for prey to die. This town *'was becoming like a ghost town'* announced The Specials during the economic recession of the early 80s. This morning commuter town Redhill, Surrey, announced itself to be in lockdown compliance.

Ghost Town was an example of a song that spoke of a certain time in history. Lyrics that mirror the socio-economic landscape in which they were written. Today I discovered that already there was a lockdown 'top 10' based on download and streaming figures. At number one it was Gerry and the Pacemakers with You'll Never Walk Alone, followed by more recent offerings from Akon with 'Locked Up' and 'Lonely'. REM has two songs in the listing, 'Everybody Hurts' and the doom laden 'It's the End of the World as we know it'. Sandwiched in between these is The Police classic, 'Don't Stand So Close To Me', ironically reflecting the social distancing 'law' we all now have to abide by.

The ironies today did not stop there. Having spent far too many hours standing too close to each other in the past weeks, our esteemed leader Boris and his Health Secretary Matt Hancock have now contracted the virus. The Chief Medical Officer is also showing symptoms and has gone into self-isolation. So, for the daily government briefing, step forward the *ever-popular* Michael Gove who at last had his chance to be top gun. Is it time for us all to go into full isolation? If I had a nuclear shelter at the bottom of the garden, then the fifty cans of beans would be stockpiled immediately.

28th March: *A Stark Choice*

As the number of people dying in the UK from Covid-19 passed 1,000, a week into lockdown had come and gone. Outside, the sun looked down from the heavens to taunt us once again - *'the weather's fine, go out and play. you won't be caught, go outside, leave your homes, no-one will know....'* Every day, it seems pictures of those doing just that are on social media, either caught in the act by high flying drones or by police helicopters. In this suburban home though, we are sitting tight, as the still surreal situation escalated to new grim heights in Italy, Spain and across the Atlantic in New York.

Diana and I remind ourselves each day, how blessed we are to have a roomy house with a large back garden, while many others are trapped in cramped accommodation. We can enjoy a patio leading up to a three-level lawn area with an extended wild jungle to the rear which separates us from a normally busy road. Jess the Cockerpoo loves her garden and first thing in the morning, and last thing at night she runs to every part of it, barking heartedly to remind the blackbirds, robins, squirrels and foxes whose territory it is. Apologies to our neighbours, the *little monster*.

This morning we sat out in the warming sunlight, sipped tea and studied the natural world around us. The newest residents, a pair of wood pigeons nesting in an ivy cloaked poplar, carried twigs back and forth to construct their nest. A pair of chaffinches, with yellow bellies and crimson head colouring helped themselves to seeds from the wired birdfeeder. In the distance a woodpecker tapped in rhythm against a nearby fence, and soaring high above, buzzards scanned the landscape for potential prey.

Nature was reminding us that despite our superiority in every aspect of earthly life, human beings are not as clever as we think we are. We are at the mercy of Mother Nature and her environment like never before - the winds that scatter us, the rains that crash through our flood defences, the heat that dries our crops and scorches the skin. We are it seems seldom in control. Now as another great pandemic humbles us, paralysing a third of the planet into hiding, we have a stark choice to make as a human race. Do we see this virus as an inconvenience, a blot in the history books after which nothing will change? Or do we see it as an opportunity to alter how we think, feel and act? A tragic event in 2020 that brings us closer together and gives us a greater sense of who we are and how we should be caring better for our natural world? One of the great writers of the C20th understood how the event of war could provide such an opportunity. In 1942, he wrote words that resonate with us today:

Satan: *'I will cause anxiety fear and panic. I will shut down schools, places of worship and sports events. I will cause economic turmoil'*

Jesus: *'I will bring together neighbours, restore the family unit. I will bring dinner back to the kitchen table. I will help people slow down their lives and appreciate what really matters. I will teach my children to rely on me and not the world. I will teach my children to trust me and not their money and their material resources'* – CS Lewis

29th March: *Adaptation*

> "It is not the strongest of the species that survives, nor the most intelligent that survives. It is the one that is the most adaptable to change."
> (quoted from Charles Darwin's Origin of Species)

I sent this quote to a senior manager of the college where I worked at the beginning of March. I was referring to the way in which I felt *structures, processes and decisions* in the organisation were too set in stone, and therefore we were in danger of falling behind the times. In particular, I pointed to the lack of digital learning provision for both staff and students, and the over-reliance on data to inform strategy rather than other forms of evidence. Looking back now at the end of the month, these words seem almost prophetic - sadly. Four weeks on, from looking forward at possibilities in the everyday course of life, to today, working through the challenge of the here and now. 'Adaptation' for everyday living has suddenly become our new frame of reference.

Here at the family ranch we are doing our best. Radio presenter Stepson has converted his bedroom into a recording studio so he can voice track his shows without going into London. The wife has transformed into a Monty Don-type goddess, scuttling around the garden like there is no tomorrow. Stepdaughter Sarah, struggling a little as many come-back-to-your-family university students do, has ploughed head first into cooking cakes and using a make-shift garden gym. My 16-year-old, *'GCSEs are now cancelled Dad, what's the point?'* son, has made the ultimate teenage boy sacrifice of being up daily at 10 O'clock each day and limited to three hours of Xbox every evening. I have adapted of course by wearing a super-resilience suit (*no capes darling*), smiling like a Cheshire, and telling everyone that *you are all doing great*. It is what alpha males do in times of crises. It must be part of our Neanderthal DNA, right? Diana has just read this over my shoulder and laughed. "No darling, DNA does not stand for *Definitely Not an Alpha*."

Even our Baptist Church has adapted. Like all places of worship, the doors are firmly shut, and the only way to reach the flock is by technology. Thankfully, we have several bright sparks in the congregation who have put their heads together on this. The result: an on-line Community Response Team who can support those who are self-isolating at the drop of a hat; or a click on the church Facebook page. *And* on Sunday mornings, like today, we can watch a full hour service on screen in the comfort of our living rooms.

The Senior Pastor, Graham, delivered the sermon this week from his back garden. A noble effort, recounting the significance of the Prodigal Son, interrupted only by freight lorries as they roared passed along the road behind the Manse. The best moment though was when 85-year-old Ethel sent three floating hearts and a smiley face emoji onto the communal screen. A new kind of digital native has been born.

Oh, the ironies just keep coming. I have just discovered on-line that Charles Darwin probably did not say those words I quoted above, and they cannot be found in his famous book. It is more likely they were first uttered by a certain Louisiana State University professor named Leon C. Megginson in 1963, from his speech delivered at the Social Science Association. He was paraphrasing Darwin's work on evolution, *adapting* the words to suit his own audience. I apologise sincerely for this fake news. I will try harder.

30th March: *Stranded*

The big government message this afternoon was aimed at calming the nerves of those who have loved ones stranded abroad. Although many thousands have been repatriated in the last few weeks, there remain tens of thousands more stuck in hotels, apartments, camp-sites and private accommodation all over the globe. It is estimated over half a million Britons have not been able to find the means to fly back. Approximately 30,000 in Australia alone are enduring the holiday from hell. Running short of money, and short of medicines in the more drastic cases, hundreds of posts and videos flood social media everyday voicing frustration from the four corners of the globe. The Foreign Office (FO) situated in King Charles Street, London, is normally resourced to cater for two major incidents at the same time such as the effects of a tsunami, rather than respond to a worldwide pandemic. Spread thinly across the six continents, the FO does not have the influence that many believe - a possible leftover perception from the power of Empire. Former Tory foreign secretary, William Hague famously noted that Kent County Council had a larger budget than the Foreign Office.

The rescue package announced would be a pledge of £75m to charter special flights to bring UK nationals home, where the few remaining commercial flights are unavailable. What seems like a random collection of airlines have signed a memorandum to work with the government to 'bring the Brits home'. However, the task of doing so would still involve negotiations with overseas territories who have shut borders, and dealing with the red tape of local airport hubs, who ceased to operate weeks ago. My heart went out to the elderly, sick and vulnerable sitting isolated in hotel rooms fearing the worst; totally hopeless far, far from home. *At home* though, a story of hope and endeavour has unfolded before our eyes.

Nearly two hundred years ago to the day a woman was born in Italy, named after the city of her birth. Called by God at the age of 17 she embarked on a life of service to others, and despite her parents' opposition, went against social convention for a young woman coming from privileged status and entered the field of nursing. A slender graceful woman she rejected potential suitors to enhance her chosen profession, becoming an influential figure in the reform of nursing both prior to and during the Crimean War in the 1850s. It was at this time that 'the lady with the lamp' became a household name. Caring for the sick and wounded on the front line with her team of highly trained nurses, she implemented new hygiene rules on handwashing and improved ventilation in field hospitals. Her legacy can be seen in the training of nurses around the world, and in March 2020 a new temporary hospital to cater for an expected four thousand people with coronavirus has been built in her name.

Christened NHS Nightingale, the transformation of the ExCel in the Docklands is testament to the hard work of planners, construction workers and medical teams. Basically, it is a field hospital of huge magnitude built in a week to nurse those who have a fighting chance of full recovery from the virus. It will bring hope to many in the coming weeks. Florence would be very proud.

31st March: *Origins*

Originating from the Greek 'pan' meaning *all* and 'demos' meaning *people*, the word pandemic refers to a disease, that according to the on-line dictionary, *is prevalent over a whole country or the world*. Today, I will just leave you with the following statistics and facts of where we are at in the war against Covid-19, taken straight off a BBC news stream:
1. US death toll - 3,415 - now larger than China's.
2. UK must go "further, faster" to ramp up coronavirus testing capacity, UK cabinet minister says.
3. A total of 1,789 people have died in the UK as of 17:00 BST on 30 March – a rise of 381.
4. American Airlines, one of the world's richest carriers, to apply for $12bn (£9.7bn) in government aid.
5. Global cases more than 800,000, with 38,000 dead; 170,000 have recovered.
6. Spain records highest number of fatalities in a single day - 849.
7. World Bank says "significant economic pain seems unavoidable" in the Asia Pacific region.

The dictionary then gives several synonyms for the word *pandemic.*

Widespread   Prevalent   Persuasive   Rife   Rampant   Global

Or as a paramedic friend of my stepson said this evening after another long shift....... 'hell'.

# April 2020

1st April: *Slow Motion*

Yesterday evening Diana and I had a wildlife bonding session on the sofa. This was partly because there seemed to be nothing else to watch on TV, and our final choice of viewing probably reflects our inner disappointment of not flying out to Cape Town this week. As for many, this holiday we had so looked forward to for months, became another victim of the pandemic.

The programme centred on Longleat Safari Park, and in particular, on the Park's one aged elephant called Anne. At over 50 years old, this gentle giant had spent most of her life at the circus before being rescued by Longleat for a well-deserved retirement. In 2015 Anne moved into a new luxurious purpose-built home giving her 24-hour access to a large outside area. Deep sandy floors, skylights and an automatic feeding system keep Anne in relative comfort. Although we were told she now takes refuge indoors most days, to the dismay of the paying public as they strain their eyes for a glimpse of Anne some twenty metres away in their cars.

In the programme the keepers were helping Anne to strengthen her 4,000 trunk muscles by laying out a carefully placed selection of bamboo shoots in the outdoor area. Gracefully, Anne emerged from her palace abode, one foot feeling for the ground before the next foot moved to catch up. A sloth-like behemoth trundling along in the slow lane of life. It was compelling viewing for animal lovers. Anne eventually finding the nourishment, using her trunk to wrap around the shoots before shoving them into her gaping mouth.

We also have an animal living in the house who moves with the same listlessness. As well as Mo, our seven year old Maine Coon cat - the one that Jess loves to chase around the ground floor - we have an old short haired tabby. At fifteen years old, Lottie now lives permanently upstairs moving from the bathroom where she feeds and poos (sometimes in the litter tray), and the hallway where she sleeps in a cocoon basket. She has lost an eye, has arthritis in at least three legs, suffers from liver disease, and a cough spurts from her mouth which sounds like a strangled mouse. It is fair to say that Lottie has used up all her nine lives and we are just waiting for the inevitable. Well, so we thought.

Three days ago, with Jess tucked up in her crate, Mo appeared like clockwork and regained control of the lounge, curling up next to me on his favourite armchair. Ten minutes later there was a scrapping at the lounge door. To everyone's surprise, Lottie nudged it open and meandered in as if drunk on vodka. Our eyes fixed on this ailing creature as she painfully navigated the coffee table and headed for the tiled corridor leading to the kitchen. A few seconds later, she returned. No-one spoke as she crashed into the sofa, recovered, and found the bottom of the stairs via the hallway. As if that was not gruesome viewing enough, I will not entreat you with the description of her eight minute ascent of the stairs. Back in the lounge we stared at each other in silence. *Was that..? Did she....? How did she climb the...? What was in the camomile tea?* Amazingly enough, Lottie has carried off this feat over the last two evenings, and we are still scratching our heads trying to understand the meaning of this ritual of endurance.

Talking of slow and painful. Diana has finally finished the greenhouse. It has taken a week to erect this 6m x 4m outdoor homage to the gardening gods. The same time it took to build NHS Nightingale in fact! Still the good news is that the swear box I placed next to the construction site is full of pound coins. Mrs B, wash your mouth out....and let us thank the Lord it is now done. Amen.

4th April : *Vital signs*

The past three days have been a whirlwind. In lockdown land this means events have taken their toll on the body and mind. For the country, this has meant another harsh dose of Covid-19. Over 4,000 have now lost their life in the UK, including a 13-year-old boy, two doctors, two nurses, and today a 5 year old hit the headlines as one of 700 more deaths on our proverbial doorstep. On Thursday, we clapped again on our actual doorsteps for the frontline workers who risk everything to keep the losses down. Abroad, Italy, Spain and the Eastern Seaboard of the USA are losing several hundred a day too. One medical scientist talked about 'nearing the peak', another mentioned something about a 'plateau in the numbers', but these words are lost in the storm that rages out of the TV screen and into our living rooms.

On Thursday, a short sharp imperfect storm landed on my lap. A reminder that on a regular basis my own health is not as it should be. Every now and then my stomach just stops doing what it should be doing. The cramps of pain turn into inflammation which turn into waves of worry. I try not to tap into the sense of anxiousness each time this happens, but perhaps inevitably I drift back to the Spring of 2017. After a day in London with Diana I knew something was not right. Pain and nausea, I had not felt before, a twisting sensation in the gut, and energy sapping out of me like the water of life draining out from a sieve.

Waking that night at twelve in a pool of sweat, I staggered to the bathroom to be sick. The last thing I remember was staring into the toilet. The paramedics arrived as I came round after spending twenty minutes sprawled across the bathroom floor. Vital signs were hardly off the scale and I insisted I was fine. *Must be just a stomach bug.* A fresh-faced paramedic called Rachel suggested a trip to A&E was advised since I had lost consciousness. I reluctantly dressed and took my first ride in an ambulance. Even then I did not know that young Rachel had probably saved my life. An hour after admission, I started wrenching, and within seconds my blood pressure was dangerously low. It was the start of sceptic shock, and once stabilised with tubes and monitors, x-rays confirmed gases were slipping through my stomach wall into my organs.

The consultant wheeled me into the operating theatre to assess the damage, telling me to expect a fight ahead. In the morning I found myself in recovery, but not in the ICU, but on a trolley bed in the corner of a very busy Outpatients Emergency area. *You were very ill Mr Banthorpe, but we couldn't find what we expected.* Diana sat at my bedside two days later when a place on a ward became available. *Did you know how hard I prayed when you went into that nose-dive?* she said. I was discharged after just three nights once my blood count returned to normal.

Unfortunately, the legacy of that experience remains. A further collapse later that year, more investigations, and several visits to East Surrey Hospital every time my stomach looked like a small hillock, took its toll on my mind as much as the internal workings of my intestines. A bit out of the blue, my stomach decided to rebel two days ago, and although I know it would sort itself out, the mind likes to play tricks. Illness turns us inwards, and the outside world fades from view. Pain has a habit of humbling the ego and making us selfish at the same time.

Tonight, as the swelling subsides, my mind turns back to that young paramedic who did her job well that night. Since then I have been in awe at what they contend with, often relatively young and newly trained, they see things every week that the rest of us never wish to see in our lifetime. Tonight, they are on the frontline again, but this time the rules of engagement have changed. This time Rachel, wherever she is, and her fellow paramedics are literally putting their own lives at risk to save ours. I prayed for their wellbeing. Paramedics – in the long nights ahead, may God protect your vital signs, as once He protected mine.

5th April: *Queen of Hearts*

The family BBQ had been a success. We sat around the patio table enjoying the slowness of the day. Chatting about the things we should be doing, applauding the efforts of my stepson's culinary skills with the naked flame. This time spent together was one of the slender sheaths of silver lining which sat against the backdrop of a very dark cloud.

Late afternoon I found myself alone in the garden. I looked up to see a solitary plane move across the cloudless sky. Two parallel white lines trailed its wake as it glided effortlessly through the stratosphere. Where had it come from, and where was it going, I thought? It was too high for the London airports – so perhaps passing through British airspace trying to reach the silhouette of the moon that sat hanging to my right. Eventually the plane shrank from view and the ghost moon remained alone once more. I considered the notion of our planet becoming uninhabitable, the moon our only sanctuary. My imagination influenced by too many Boys Own sci-fi books in my youth perhaps. By too many Hollywood movies about pandemics and zombies since.

At eight O'clock the country sat down to tune into a special broadcast. It was only the fifth time in her 67-year reign that the Queen has spoken to the nation in this way, outside of the traditional Christmas greeting. In the pre-recording she spoke with a tour de force you would not expect from a 93-year-old. She thanked NHS staff, and all those who were working to keep key services moving. She praised the British spirit and referred back inevitably to wartime. She looked squarely into the camera and told us we would all get through this, and though separated from family and friends for now, we would one day *meet again*. You could almost hear Dame Vera in the background echoing the sentiments in perfect tune; and in the mind's eye pictures of White Cliffs appeared, sweeping and broad, protecting us from the unseen enemy. It was a stirring and inspirational speech. *Our Queen*, the only monarch most of us have ever known, meeting us right in the heart of battle.

2000 years ago they shouted 'messiah' and 'saviour' as he entered Jerusalem on a colt. Palm leaves lay across the dusty streets to welcome him into the great ancient city. The crowds thought he would free them from Roman rule so they could return to lives lost since the occupation of their land. They were up for the fight and their king had arrived. In the shadows, figures of authority started to whisper and scheme, for this *king* had just ridden into their lair. Let the battle commence.

7th April: *Resilience*

It seems to be one of the buzzwords of the new decade - *'resilience'*. The growth in mental health awareness, certainly in the UK, has led to a vast library of academic papers, tabloid articles and read-the-guru textbooks on the subject. In my field of education, I fell into this bandwagon by chance, ending up writing a national project paper on the mindfulness and well-being of teachers in Further Education. Along the way, I moved from one of those people who thought 'it's a teens thing - a fad of the age' to 'yeah, I get it. We all need mental and emotional support in the same way we focus on physical health'. So now it is one of my key mantras in the workplace - look after your teachers, and they will then have the well-being capacity to look after those in their professional care. In my presentations to staff I refer to familiar on-board aircraft instructions to highlight the point; *in the case of low cabin pressure adults to put on their oxygen masks first before fitting the child's mask concept.*

One of the strategies to support good mental health and well-being is to look at how any individual can build up their 'resilience' mechanisms. I stress this has nothing to do with developing a 'British stiff upper lip', take the hard knocks, dust yourself down, *keep calm and carry on teaching*. It is more about how as humans we cope with change. Finding 'acceptance' of the things we cannot control, and working towards bettering the things we can change is a great place to start. So, in the centre of the storm, how do we cope? Denial? Anger? Rebellion? Fight? Flight?

Lockdown week three in the UK. A rise in the sale of alcohol and an increase in domestic violence are already concerning trends. The strain on relationships in some families known to us is starting to show. Loved ones and partners separated by distance can go one of two ways. Sadly, Dan and his girlfriend could not find the common ground to keep their relationship alive after two years. Living 35 miles apart in a pandemic was the straw that broke cupid's back. In the midst of a pandemic, the stress in trying to keep things going was the uncontrollable factor which was almost inevitably accepted by each.

Thankfully, our flop-haired PM Boris, is showing great fight and personal resilience as he spends a second night in St Thomas' with Covid-19. Irrespective of political persuasion the thoughts of all are with him. His pregnant partner has thankfully recovered her health. A little more good news - my parents celebrated their 57th wedding anniversary. They were able to have a nice self-isolation meal together. 'Luckily I found a piece of lamb in the freezer' Mum declared to the world. Lucky old Dad, *meat and two veg again*. At 87 he still has a lovely touch of East End humour - *'it's our Heinz anniversary'* he noted on the phone. He'd waited 57 years for that joke. Bless him. A man married to my mother for that long? Now that's resilience.

8th April: *Rainbows*

Walking our cockerpoo Jess has become the mainstay exercise for the five of us. Yes, we are blessed to have a large garden, in which the wife spends several hours a day doing a good impression of Charlie Dimmock on steroids; but it is good just to get out. Within the government guideline restrictions of course, so that's 'once around the block' with Jess taking about 10 minutes. Or 5 minutes if young Daniel's turn, as he literally drags the poor dog around the roads in haste, before resuming his school homework on XBox.

Today, as I took the late afternoon 'walkies' shift I noticed how many rainbows there were in house windows - presumably drawn by primary school children. This symbol has become one of the themes of the current crises, starting in Italy and Spain, and then taken on initially by school teachers here to give their pupils a focus of hope for the future. The subsequent flow of rainbow creations is now booming across the nation, the seven distinct colours appearing in a wide range of formats, from ceramics, patchwork, and metal to coloured arches made from foodstuffs.

Yet in all the coverage on this phenomenon there is not one reference to the Biblical symbolism of the rainbow. In Genesis, the rainbow signifies God's promise never to flood the Earth again to rid the world of sin. In this famous story, only Noah and his family got the heads up from above and built the ark which carried them eventually to safe ground. A great story... a great Sunday School story whether you believe it happened or not.

Genesis tells us the rainbow is God's symbol of hope - a promise that his anger would never strike again in the same way. Though in recent memory we *have* seen great floods, and tsunamis of destruction crushing everything in their path. I was in Sri Lanka several years after the 2004 tidal wave, and the devastation to land and community was still there to be seen. We have seen earthquakes, volcanoes and bushfires do their worst to man and beast, and we have had diseases decimating populations in Africa and Asia. We recall the last widespread contagion that plagued the continent of Europe and beyond. Between 1918 and 1920 the so-called Spanish flu infected 500 million people, or around 25% of the world's population at the time. The death toll estimate was up to 50 million, with some experts saying double that. Wow - that's a pandemic! Apocalyptic in nature, the religious soothsayers argued at the time, and since.

One hundred years later, despite the huge advances in medical science, we are at the mercy of a worldwide plague once more. A virus without boundaries. So, God has in effect kept His promise - no flood yet to wipe out the whole of humanity. You have to go to the other end of the Bible to pick up the thread. In Revelation we are told how pestilence and disease will sweep through the nations, accompanied by plagues of locust and large crop destruction. The latter is happening now in Eastern Africa. The UN has just issued a warning that swarms of locusts the size of cities are on the march. These are dark times, in which searching for light in that darkness becomes the human default position.

Initially that search of hope rests on the shoulders of scientists as they strive to find a vaccine. Those of us with belief in an Almighty God will seek light through a call to prayer. Prayer, it could be argued is faith in action, built around an acceptance of who God is and who we are not. When it comes to facing an Armageddon of locusts, the best thing to do I humbly suggest is to accept our limitations and kneel. The next time I take Jess around the block, I will count the rainbows, count my own blessings, and pray for mercy.

10th April: *Lottie*

Easter is my favourite time of the year. As well as being a significant time for Christians, I particularly love the seasonal changes that occur all around us. The spray of colours, the sight and sound of garden birds flourishing in our suburban gardens, the warmth of the low evening sun and last but not least, two weeks off work from the world of education. Good Friday usually starts with a march of witness through the local town - churches united in their reverence to Christ's crucifixion. This is followed by a family lunch and a relaxing day, normally orientated around a long dog walk. But there is nothing normal about Good Friday 2020.

As if today was going to be strange enough, I am woken at 7 a.m. by a high-pitched cry. A noise I do not recognise. Blurry eyed my feet find the bedroom floor. Diana stirs, but remains asleep. On the upstairs landing I find Lottie lying on the carpet in obvious distress and pain. You remember Lottie, the one-eyed tabby with every cat condition you can name? Over the last week her health has obviously deteriorated further, but somehow she had found the determination to keep visiting us in the lounge. And to greater surprise, two days ago she lay in the front garden under her favourite cedar tree keeping green fingered Diana company for several hours. Now, hardly breathing and pleading for her human family to do something to end the pain, Lottie held it together in time for all to get up and say goodbye. Thankfully, the local vets quickly lightened the burden and Lottie went to cat heaven within the hour. At our fish BBQ later in the day we toasted Lottie's life. When it came to resilience this cat had it in abundance. A fighter to the last.

However sad losing a domestic pet is, we also knew that our grief was nothing compared to those who were losing family and friends every day to Covid-19. In the last 24 hours in the UK another 980 people had lost their fight for life. A total of nearly 10,000. Globally, the Johns Hopkins University now say over 100,000 deaths have been recorded as a direct result of the virus. Staggering and unsettling. Yet, if we can move from our Eurocentric perspective of the world, one eye is on those countries which are barely on the upward death curve. South America, Africa, India and other parts of Asia await with bated breath. The fear is that the numbers in Europe will pale into insignificance once the touch paper is lit in places where ventilators and other emergency equipment are scarce.

On this 'Good' Friday, a term derived from C13th English word 'goude' meaning 'holy', the Christian message seems lost. Not meeting as a collective force for hope in towns across the world has left me feeling empty. On-line pulpit messages were there, but this was not a substitute for the power of communal fellowship. Today the global Church of Christ did not have a spring in its step. At a time like this we need visible Christian leadership. We need to meet this crisis head on with a spiritual resilience not seen in modern history. Rest in peace Lottie. Today you reminded us that determination and fortitude are key gifts of the human spirit.

12th April: *The Portabella Priest*

Easter Sunday. Up to 23 degrees in the Home Counties, and the police are out in force to ensure we keep social distancing a top priority. Again, I feel for those living in cramped accommodation spaces, and without even a small garden to soak in the warmth of the sun and the fresh air. The large London parks thankfully remain open. Hyde, Regent's and St James' were being well used by walkers, runners, and cyclists. These huge open spaces were created by the Victorians to be the 'lungs' of London, a chance for the capital's residents to escape the foul stench of the overpopulated streets. Today, they are serving a different but no less significant purpose.

Closer to home the local parks and wooded areas are soon busy. My stepson lost count of the family groups he passed as he enjoyed his daily jog around the nearby landscape. Three weeks into our lockdown and confined by the same walls is a mental struggle. In some European countries they are starting to talk about 'numbers peaking' or 'reaching a plateau on the curve'. Spain, one of the worst hit countries will allow essential workers back in offices and building sites tomorrow. However, The World Health Organisation (WHO) are concerned that relaxing lockdowns too early will cause secondary waves of infections and prolong the agony. Every day in the UK the Government is asked when our lockdown will end. *No time soon* is the response. Mixed international messages in a global crisis is not helpful.

I am pleased that today there are no mixed messages from the church on the most significant day in the Christian calendar. The Pope gave mass in a near empty St Peter's Basilica and carried on his message from his earlier Easter vigil service, urging people not to 'yield to fear' but be 'messengers of life in a time of death'. He echoed the story of the empty tomb, when initial fear turned to hope through Christ's resurrection. The Archbishop of Canterbury Justin Welby preached from his kitchen table. 'We cannot be content to go back to what was before' he said, 'in a time of uncertainty, fear, despair and isolation...in the resurrection we have a hope that is surer than stone'. Diana and I were able to meet with many of our church friends via Zoom this morning after our on-line service. This was the church being adaptable and resilient, a far cry from the silence of Good Friday.

However, the story that touched my heart the most was that of Pat Allerton, the vicar of St Peter's, Notting Hill, also known as 'The Portobello Priest'. During the lockdown Pat has decided if Mohammed cannot come to the mountain, then the mountain must go to Mohammed. Ok, mixed religious metaphors is not helpful either, but you know what I mean. Everyday Pat drives to a different street and holds a 10 minute service using a loudspeaker system fixed inside the boot of his car. Nearby residents sing along to Amazing Grace and join in the Lord's Prayer from doorsteps and windows.

This reminded me that 'church' is not a building but the collection of believers and worshippers who meet together within it. On-line via the internet, using apps like Zoom, in the streets and in our homes; the old world meeting the new. As Pope Francis highlighted today, we need unity more than ever. We need a clear message of faith, hope and renewal directed at the hearts and minds of all nations. We certainly need more people with the practical conviction of The Portobello Priest.

14th April: *A Dogs Life*

I know I don't know much. I am young but not as young as I was. I think I am learning new things every day but I'm not sure if they are new or not? Life is exciting but sometimes I do get very confused about what is going on. There are things I know I really like to do. I like getting up in the morning with *Daddy*. *Daddy* takes me in *garden* to go *pee-pee* and *poo-poo*. Then I have my *num-nums* in *kitchen*. *Daddy* leaves me behind *gate* and takes *mummy tea*. I wait nicely...but if I find something to chew then that makes waiting nicer. I like to chew *shoes* most.

Then *mummy* takes me *walkies*. I love *walkies* but this is where I have started to get confused. I am sure I like *walkies* to *park* and *woods,* but I do not go there now. I go *walkies* around *block* every day. Actually, I just go *walkies* around *block* but with someone different each time. I go with *Mummy, Daddy, Daniel*, there's another smaller *Daniel* too - but he walks very fast! Sometimes I go *walkies* with *Sarah* and she speaks to someone called *Owen* who lives in a small box in her hand.

I get tired from *walkies* around *block*. I miss *park*. I remember meeting friends of mine too. There's one called *Fozzie*, one called *Bertie* and one called *Timmy*. I don't see them now. I must have been very *naughty*. I miss them.

I love *garden*. It is big and I run and run. My favourite game is *play ball*. I chew the *ball*. Lots of them. *Daddy* plays *big kick* with me. We play every day now.

I also see *mummy* in *garden*. I watch her do lots of things. She does *digging*. I like *digging* but *mummy* doesn't like me *digging*. She also puts *socks* up high. I jump and run off with *socks*. *Mummy* gives me a *biscuit* every time I do this. I will do this more often. It works with *shoes* too. And *plastic* bits. And anything really. I like biscuits.

I like chasing. I like chasing *ball*. But I like chasing *Mo* better. *Mo* looks a bit like me. But then perhaps not. I jump and bark, and bark louder. But

Mo will not play with me. He sometimes hits me on the nose. If I stop chasing *Mo, Daddy* gives me a *biscuit*. I will keep doing this too. There was another smaller fur-thing. She was slow and did not move at all some days. I think she was called *Lottie*. I do not see her now. Maybe she has gone to a better home.

When I am *big tired* I go to *bo-bos* in my *bed*. *Mummy and Daddy* call this *nite-nites*. *Mummy* makes nice noises to make me close my eyes. I like being me. I have lots of fun with my family. They are here every day with me now. All the time. This is nice. I want this to be my forever.

15th April: *99 Not Out*

Fundraising has become part of the fabric of postmodern society. Children in Need, Comic Relief and the London Marathon are just three of the annual fundraising events which are as much part of the calendar cycle as Guy Fawkes and Valentine's Day. Yet, every week in the UK tens of thousands of ordinary people give their time, skills and money in the support of hundreds of good causes through coffee mornings, jumble sales and fun runs. A shout out too for the Postcode Lottery and the National Lottery, which although some may consider as gambling through the back door, have both raised millions for charities in their time.

During the Covid-19 pandemic raising money to support those who are in very vulnerable and complex situations has also become an essential element of lockdown. It seems that anyone who is able to contribute is trying to do their bit. So every Friday night the Banthorpe clan takes part in an on-line quiz organised by one of Dan's radio friends. All money raised goes to the Food Bank which is doing a great job supplying much needed provisions to some of the poorest in society. Our small financial contribution is not going to rock the planet but the combined effort of over twenty teams quizzing their little hearts out each week will see the overall total swiftly rise.

Over the past week however, a story has emerged that puts our meagre contributions into perspective. There are some things that can only happen in Britain, and this is a prime example of the very *best of us*. Captain Tom Moore is a 99-year-old war veteran who started his own fundraising effort on 8th April. He hoped to raise £1,000 for NHS Charities Together by walking 100 laps of his garden. Initially he had hoped to reach this target by his 100th birthday on 30th April. Yesterday, on live TV he managed to walk the last 25 lengths, finishing the home stretch to the cheers of a guard of honour from the 1st Battalion of the Yorkshire Regiment.

Initially raising over £7,000 in the first 24 hours of his walk-a-thon, the target went to an ambitious £1m. Media coverage grew and grew, and his fundraising platform JustGiving announced this was the largest amount raised through a single campaign. The running total as of today stands at an incredible £15m. Captain Tom has indeed captured the heart of the nation. The NHS effort was being applauded again, this time in tangible pounds and pence.

Tonight, Diana and I watched an extraordinary half hour of television. Actor Ross Kemp and a camera crew had been granted unlimited access to the Intensive Care Unit of Milton Keynes University Hospital Trust. We saw patients on ventilators fighting for their lives. We saw doctors and nurses demonstrate impeccable professionalism and a great deal of love and devotion. We saw George being discharged after 13 days in the ICU and the reaction of the nurse who had looked after him in the darkest moments. One doctor pleaded with the nation to abide by the lockdown rules - *even the young and fit are dying from this*, he remonstrated. This was an insight that brought home the battle frontline into our living rooms once again. We sat watching numb and humbled. The government announced three more weeks of lockdown this afternoon, and while we grimaced at the thought, we knew in our heart of hearts this had to be the right course of action. We salute you Tom, and we continue to clap for our beloved NHS in awe and with great admiration.

17th April: *Space Oddity*

One of the advantages, if you can call it that, of being in a lockdown is having the opportunity to catch up with films and TV programmes you have been meaning to watch for ages; but never got around to it. For me and fellow sports pundit stepson Dan it has been two football fly-on-the-wall documentaries, *Sunderland* d 'Til I Die Series 2, and All or Nothing, Manchester City 2017-18 Season. For family films, it has been the all-star who dunnit Knives Out, the surreal Beatles homage Yesterday, and earlier this week, the Elton John biopic, Rocketman.

In the past few days Diana and I have revisited an old 90's favourite with a twist. *Picard*, a Netflix exclusive, and as we were reminded every time we tune in, this is a follow up narrative to Star Trek The Next Generation. In this new series we follow the exploits of Jean Luc as he wrestles with old age, reminiscing about the good old days on The US Enterprise. Patrick Stewart is as watchable as ever in the lead role, and we quickly became hooked. The gogglebox is the C21st comfort blanket, and sometimes it is just what the doctor ordered, to sit down and watch a great fictional (or science-fictional) story to take the mind off more important things. It is also comforting to reminisce, finding solace in the past when surely life was not as complex and fragile as it is now. Can I remember for instance, what life was like before Tweets, Blogs, Podcasts, Bluetooth, 3D printing, artificial intelligence, GPS, global warming and er...Netflix?

Keeping with the space theme, what was life like for the three astronauts who boarded the International Space Station in the Autumn of 2019? Well, we were Covid-19 free for a start. Yesterday Oleg Skrypochka, Andrew Morgan and Jessica Meir returned to a very different planet to the one they left 200 plus days ago. On hitting terra ferma once again, they were greeted in Kazakhstan by a mask-wearing rescue team that had previously been in strict quarantine. With all the airports closed in the country, the astronauts were taken first to a Russian owned space launch pad site. From there the Russian astronaut will take a plane directly home to his motherland, with the two

Americans driven to a NASA plane three hours distance away. The hardest change of protocol perhaps will be when they all re-unite with loved ones with social distancing rules in force. One of the Americans Jessica Meir made history in 2019 after completing the first ever all-female spacewalk with another NASA astronaut, but now she faced a 'no hugs, no contact' reunion with her family. *'I think I will feel more isolated on Earth than here'* she said on a video call before returning to Earth. Coming from a human being who has just spent 205 days far above the world sitting in a tin can, that is saying something.

18th April: *Cabin Fever*

The nation is about to start its next phase of lockdown, and the comfort of the Easter break, which for many is associated with 'time off work and school', is at an end. Today the Government announced at least three more weeks before lockdown measures will be reviewed again. The statistics of infection numbers and death rates are constantly with us. Globally, millions have now caught Covid 19, with over 150,000 recorded deaths. In mainland Europe there is hope that the worst in Italy, Spain and Germany may be over, yet hundreds are still losing their fight for life every day. In the UK, we have sadly broken the 15,000-death mark. We are told the NHS has spare capacity, with two more Nightingale Hospitals having been built in the Midlands and in the North East. Extra ventilators are forthcoming, either from abroad or through the ingenuity of hi-tech companies closer to home. However, two issues have dominated the social and political landscape in the past several days. The suspected high death count in care homes, and the lack of Protective Personal Equipment for those on the front line, both headline the hourly news. *PPE* has become a three-letter anacronym that is now as familiar as *NHS*. In vocational education we have used this term for years on lesson plans to denote health and safety requirements in practical workshops. It will never just seem like simple 'PPE' again.

Despite the distressing numbers, and the clear UK Government messages, more people are getting twitchy. *When will the lockdown end? Has the Government an exit strategy in place?* The situation is compounded with images of people being freed from isolation elsewhere. In Denmark, younger children are being sent back to schools, albeit to classes where social distancing still applies. In Spain, construction workers and other manufacturing sectors are returning to work, and in Germany Angela Merkel has announced a series of staged exit steps.

In our household the strain is also beginning to tell. The jobs and tasks that kept us busy over the past three weeks have dried up. There are only so many times you can re-organise the condiments cupboard. There is a finite limit to how many plants and vegetables one can plant in the garden. The daily walks are losing their novelty factor, and even my son has declared he is becoming bored with Xbox. There is a reference to *the end of civilisation as we know it* here, but I am trying to keep things in perspective. However, yesterday with the temperature cooling and rain falling intermittently on the newly designed herb garden, Diana and myself also had our first lockdown tiff. Well, Diana was displeased, and I listened. Accused of 'disappearing too often upstairs to do college work' and only appearing when it suited me was the gist of it. Jess the Cockerpoo also has to take some blame. Cooped up indoors for the first time in days, she has demonstrated her own version of cabin fever. Think: canine frustration, lounge carpet and heavy chewing. Diana had had enough.

So this morning with the sun back in charge of the weather, the three of us set off early to the woods for the first time in weeks. The runners, cyclists and family walking trains had not yet emerged, so we enjoyed the freedom of the labyrinthine paths. Then, after several minutes of tromping through the light fern, we reached the wood's summit, and there stretching out before us lay the reward for our labours. A carpet of bluebells unfolded like a flowing wedding train, both to our left and to our right. Hundreds of thousands of tiny flowers strewn amongst the trees, a sea of blue ebbing and flowing in the breeze. Jess of course was more interested in the multitude of smells, her snout hoovering the ground like a supercharged Dyson. It was breath-taking, and at once my mind cleared of numbers and worry, and Diana's smile returned as she forgot the stresses of the previous day.

We will return our minds to the realities of the pandemic. Yet for this hour we became trapped in the beauty of creation. Great for the mind, even better for the soul. We are so thankful for what we still have because it is so much more than what most of humanity must endure. Going back to the very essence of nature and breathing in the tranquillity which only it can bring, is a positive way to begin the next phase of this incredibly unnatural way of living.

19th April: *Bread and Wine*

Last night's family lockdown film was King of Thieves with Michael Caine leading an all-star British cast. The film recounts the 2015 Hatton Garden jewel heist in London when a group of criminals came out of retirement to carry out the 'job' they wished they had attempted decades earlier. Based on the true story of Brian Reader and his accompanying band of fellow crooks, the film explores the temptation not only of greed, but also of re-living the past. In this case the psychological *fix* of thieving, and the excitement of facing risk and danger head-on, were just too tempting a lure back to past endeavours.

Re-living the past as we grow older is something that has weighed more heavily in these days of slow-down and personal reflection. Looking back to what I could have achieved in life, or perhaps what I could have done differently, can creep up on you and twist the mind into a spiral of damaging regret. In our on-line church service this morning Senior Pastor Graham gave the viewing flock much food for thought. The Bible passage from John Chapter 21 is the account of Jesus' appearance to the disciples by the Sea of Galilee, several days after his resurrection. Unsuccessful in their trawl for fish that morning, the disciples encounter a man standing on the shore, who directs them to throw their net in a different direction. In doing so they catch a large haul and their eyes open to the risen Christ standing before them. Proclaiming him Lord, they join Jesus for a beach BBQ. Sounds idyllic.

The message? Well, Graham suggested that at this time in our lives, instead of looking back at what might have been and settling for the story and even the final chapter we feel already assigned to, could we not trust in another ending that is to come? He likened it to the Director's Cut of a film - famously engineered by Ridley Scott with his alternative ending of Blade Runner in the 1980s. We may think we have our story mapped out already, largely a sum of regrets and failings from the past. Yet God may have his own Director's Cut ready for us. *If,* and that is the challenge - *if* we can faithfully and obediently throw our nets over the other side of our boat, what would the outcome be? A walk down a different path? A step out of our comfort zone? An abundance of God's glory shown to us in full view?

As a further reminder of Christ's love for us, we celebrated communion, social distancing style. We took bread and wine (or ciabatta and a strong dose of Ribena) in our own homes, and this in itself was a special reminder how our faith is best served in the present, believing not in the historical Jesus but in the living Christ who knows what is happening now. He is with us today, ready to help us take that different path to an ending far more exciting than we can ever imagine.

Pastor Graham will not thank me for mentioning here that my favourite part of the service was the children's telling of John 21 using Lego figures, with computer pasted speech bubbles coming from the characters' mouths. Not only that, but Jesus was played by Lego Luke Skywalker with white robe and fair hair to boot! Jesus - a Jedi Knight. I knew it!!

20th April: A Bit of a Mess

'Back to work'. A Summer term of uncertainty begins for all, but perhaps especially for educators who will endeavour to strike the balance between aspiration and reality. For the younger pupils it is a combination of home schooling, BBC Bitesize on-line learning, and creative play when boredom sets in – *usually around 2 pm in the afternoon I hear*. Some funny posts on Facebook have noted parents around the world praising teachers to the hilt, with *'please take them back, you have been misunderstood*, and general *'we love teachers'* messages providing an ironic take on the situation.

Most secondary school pupils will be enticed into home learning by teachers desperate to keep in touch with a sense of 'doing the right thing'. The gold standards of our assessment laden education system, GCSEs and A Levels, have ground to a halt - no exams in June to aim for, with pupils in Year 11 and Year 13 putting down pens in favour of joysticks and iPhones. Universities are now worried about their potential intake for September. Teachers have been told to 'grade as best they can', and for those applying for a place in HE there will be a nervous wait for anyone caught out by not putting in their best shift with January's Mock A Levels. Fortunately for my Daniel, he performed well in his GCSE Mocks and has his place in sixth form guaranteed. Hence the present nonchalance and midday breakfasts.

As for the Cinderella of the education system, Further Education has been left like a lame duck on a game shoot. What to do then with technical and vocational qualifications which are delivered in a multitude of ways, subject to a myriad of assessment rules, with no 'mocks' to fall back on? How do you finish a course satisfactorily when 50% is based on practical assessment? How can you then safely progress L2 electrician students onto a L3 course in September without any confidence they can wire a plug without putting themselves and others at risk? Parallels with the 2019/20 football season here; too late to start again, and probably not enough time to fit in the matches left before the next season starts. The pandemic is making us decide between a rock and a hard place.

Anyway, to illustrate the confusion further, this morning's two-hour Microsoft Teams meeting with fellow college managers was like finding your way in the dark without a match. Questions abounded. Do we continue to provide distance learning when any new work will no longer count towards qualification achievement? Do we all just call it a day and enjoy the sunshine? To be honest it is a bit of a mess, and the losers of course are all the pupils and students who will not forget the year their education was severely interrupted by a worldwide pandemic.

In the media, the phrase 'new normal' keeps popping up. A new catchphrase for our time. Scientists have also said this could be the first of many new strains of coronavirus - type pandemics. We might even start to think of a world 'BC', Before Covid 19, and 'AC', After Covid 19. The year when everything changed. A year when we stopped worrying about which "A" level grade we achieved? What our next holiday destination could be? And how did my football team lose that match?

2,000 years ago, the world also began a *new normal*, when God set His great mission of salvation in motion. 2020 could be another defining point in history when we turn our attention back to the very essence and purpose of our existence. Maybe His story has come full circle.

22nd April: *Satellites*

Last night's family film offering was plucked from the DVD wall shelving. Well, I say 'family', it finally ended up being stepson Dan and my choice for *boys own* viewing. Diamonds are Forever was Sean Connery's last official outing as 007 in 1969. It was one the Bonds I had not seen for a while, and Dan loves everything nostalgic. For example, to relieve his lockdown boredom threshold he has just purchased a record player from Amazon. This was to accompany his other recent buys - several re-digitised LPs and a lovely record case with real retro appeal. It is quite refreshing to see a young man of 22 appreciate the finer things of the 1970s.

Anyway, back to the film. Watching this again, three things stood out for me. The hand to hand fight scenes compared badly against modern examples of moderate violence seen for instance in the Jason Bourne series or in The Transporter. Secondly, the cliché driven script - which at times was actually laugh out loud funny when I'm sure originally it was meant to be seriously dramatic. Thirdly, the characterisation of the arch villain Ernst Blofeld illustrated that *one* thing has not changed much over the past 50 years. Blofeld had money, lots of it, and with this fortune came a sense of destiny. He was the archetypal megalomaniac wielding power and influence, trying to stake his own claim on history.

Even the far more recent Daniel Craig Bond plotlines centred around the same concept, ironically with a re-packaged Blofeld for the 21st Century, engineering dastardly schemes in each of Craig's five outings as the superspy. The world has always had its share of Blofelds. In the real world, the same wealthy influencers exist to exert their own blueprint on society. Business entrepreneurs such as Mark Zuckerberg and Bill Gates have become as famous as the brands they created. Politicians continue to mix state duties with outside business ventures to gain further influence and power. Would you be surprised if I told you Vladimir Putin can be found in Forbes top 10 richest persons on the planet list?

60th on the list, worth upwards of $20bn, is another famous businessman, Elon Musk. A great name for a Bond villain with egotistical ambitions to match some of the most noteworthy Ian Fleming creations - Dr No, Auric Goldfinger, Max Zorin, Hugo Drax, Elliot Carver to name a few. In fact, the comparison between Drax (Moonraker) and Elon Musk was visible in the night sky this week. Chief Executive of SpaceX, Musk has been launching large batches of satellites for several weeks to apparently improve global internet coverage. Eventually 12,000 of them will move further away from Earth's orbit and beam enhanced broadband into our homes. As instructed by social media messages, the five of us stood obediently in the garden straining necks backwards to view the clear cosmos above. After several false sightings, we spotted tiny lights moving rapidly from West to East. Not something you see every day - impressive in both technology and visual impact. Billions spent on thousands of satellites, moving under the constellations like branded shooting stars.

Today there was a stark warning from the Executive Director of the World Food Programme. He was reported as saying the world is heading for a 'famine of Biblical proportions' if Western governments do not act fast to protect food supplies in developing countries during the pandemic. David Beasley is concerned the impact of any shrinking of national output in wealthy nations will result in a reduction in financial capacity to support food chains elsewhere. A UN report notes the number of people with acute food insecurity is expected to rise from 135 million to 265 million by the end of 2020. This certainly puts other pandemic statistics in the shade and puts our need for toilet paper and pubs into perspective. It would seem Covid-19 is exposing inequality at all levels - wealth, access, race, education etc. etc. Watching tiny satellites race across the sky funded by a multi-billionaire when millions could soon die of starvation pretty much sums up a divide as wide as the cosmos itself.

23rd April: *Am I Bovverred?*

One of the most stressful parts of lockdown is the big family shop. Every week Diana and I sit down and do a thorough risk analysis on what we need, and more importantly, what the chances are of making it *out* without contagion. We have managed to find a rationale to shop at every available option in the locality. Redhill Sainsburys - *potential car park gridlock, trolley fill up can take forever, long check out queues*; Redhill Priory Farm - *small, less busy between 10.30 and 10.45, very expensive*; Redhill Co-op - *moderate size, can be empty, less chance of finding Kellogg's Special K*; Reigate Morrisons - *familiar, easy parking, narrow isles*; Turner's Corner shop down the road - *quick service, only sells toilet roll and BBQ lighters.*

As most shops only let in one person at a time it is a toss-up between the two of us. We have asked the three off-springs to offer their services but have all declined citing 'I'm revising for exams'; 'I'm recording three radio shows at the moment'; and 'I'm too young to die'. I think my son needs to grow up a bit. As I am technically the most immune vulnerable, and because Diana does not trust me to know the difference between Quorn and corn, then it is my good lady wife who carries the shopping burden. Of course, I am there at the end to help carry the bags to the car, but I will accept who is at the sharp end of the deal here. Joking apart, Diana comes back emotionally drained from the 2 meter separation queuing, the jostling for isle position, and the pressure of adhering to the 'list', half of which appears on her family WhatsApp as she navigates the trolley around other nervous shoppers. Woe betide anyone who questions the outcome of her endeavours! *'Oh Mum, you forgot the Peri-Peri sauce'* for want of a better term, goes down like the plague.

The aftermath of the big shopping trip is now set in stone. Two mature adults and three gannets living in the house means the food stock diminishes at an alarming rate. Periods of idleness or boredom signify the cause, and long rummage in the cupboards or the fridge, the 'effect'. The first to go are the chocolate bars, followed by the cereal, and the dishwasher is full every night with 19 glasses, as every drop of liquid is consumed like water flowing down a drain. A silly Facebook caption suggesting 100% of the family budget now goes on food during lockdown for us is not far off the mark.

'They just treat home like a BnB' remarks Diana almost daily. 'Your Dan gets up at midday, eats, plays Xbox, eats, plays Xbox till midnight, eats, sleeps..'....'...and dreams of playing Xbox.'. I know, my darling' I add.' And your Dan thinks a light snack is half a buffalo, a bucket of chips and an allotment of veg as a side!' Happy days. Again, I think of the famine forecast by the UN this week for developing countries. We so easily fall into the comfort trappings of Western living. We ARE so blessed with a full fridge and a cupboard of produce that most families will never be able to afford. This bothers me more than ever.

Tonight, Children in Need and Comic Relief banded together to bring us three hours of entertainment. It's a mix of live and recorded music, comedy and high jinx from some of the nation's new and established talent. It was great to see Dawn French as The Vicar of Dibley once again, David Walliams and Matt Lucas reprise their characters from Little Britain, and perhaps the highlight for me was Katherine Tate back as the crassly funny Lauren, winding up her teacher played brilliantly by David Tennant. Lauren's memorable catch phrase is 'am I bovvered?' - a dismissive phrase of frustrated youth and teen apathy. And this was the pertinent question of the whole night. *Were we bothered?* Snugged up in our living rooms munching Pringles and sipping glasses of sparkling something.

We were subjected to images of young, often very sick, people who have been gravely affected by the lockdown, stories of charities who need extra funds to cope, and pleas from those working on the front line putting their lives at risk.

Were we bovvered? £27m raised in under three hours suggests a lot of people are. In the scheme of things, a drop in the ocean, but despite five weeks of social incarceration, the great British public spirit is very much alive and kicking.

25th April: *Milestones*

Today's headlines were dominated by unwanted statistics yet again. At the daily government news briefing, the Home Secretary Priti Patel announced what she described as a 'tragic and terrible milestone'. The latest figures showed that more than 20,000 people had died with Covid-19 in UK hospitals, 51 days after the first virus related death had been reported. This total was of particular importance, because the government's chief scientific advisor stated in March that keeping the death toll below 20,000 would be a 'good outcome'. These figures do not even account for deaths in care homes, at home, in hospices or elsewhere in the community. It made sombre viewing.

The worldwide virus death toll also reached a grim milestone. More than 200,000 people have now lost their lives to Covid-19, with nearing 3 million confirmed cases in 210 countries (Johns Hopkins University). Apart from the UK, the other countries with over 20,000 deaths are Italy, Spain, France and the US. The United States alone had now recorded over 50,000 deaths. Even with some commentators and experts noting the worst may be over in Western Europe, this week the World Health Organisation highlighted upwards trends in Africa, Eastern Europe, Central America and South America. India, with a population of nearly 1.4 billion, is holding its breath as cases begin to creep upwards, despite a stringent three-week lockdown.

Large numbers. Big milestones in the battle against Covid-19. Behind the statistics lie personal tragedies, grieving families and stories of courage and sacrifice. As the weeks move on, these stories are edging closer to home. Our neighbour's grandmother died in the past couple of days. Big Dan's friend's father lies in a coma in East Surrey Hospital, a paramedic fighting for his life. Reminders of mortality and lives cut short with little warning. Reminders that Covid-19 does not discriminate and fears no borders. For many, fear has become a daily routine.

As a Christian, the most significant milestone in my life was the day I gave myself to Christ. This remains the best decision I ever made.

Through the years, I have known deep personal challenge and found myself in some very dark places. Yet God has been merciful, taking me through each stage of my Christian journey with patience and compassion. In the darkest of all places, facing death, he replaced my fear with faith. He turned despair into hope, and in doing so gave me so many opportunities to live under Christ's power and grace. In the Bible, Jesus is referred to as the 'cornerstone' of life, the foundation on which all else is built upon. It is this belief that keeps me secure in God's plan for my life, and His plan for the whole world.

Tonight, I pray for those who feel alone and scared. For those who fear the unknown of this life and the next. I pray for this nation. I pray for forgiveness for the way we have worshipped the idols of money, materialism, and greed. I pray for repentance - and a chance to open our hearts and minds to the One who holds us in the palm of His hands. I pray that this moment in our history becomes a milestone for revival. God in heaven, we need you to be our most precious milestone and our eternal cornerstone.

26th April: *In Denial*

Today was meant to be marathon day in London. Approximately 26 miles run on the 26th of the month. So some bright spark in marketing came up with The 2.6 Challenge. Why not *The 26 Challenge*? Perhaps decimals are the new whole numbers? Anyway, this is for a good cause, a nationally promoted campaign to replace one of the biggest one-day fundraising events in the British calendar. Last year in fact, The London Marathon raised more than £66.4 million for thousands of charities. With many smaller charities reducing or even stopping their services in recent weeks, this was a chance for everyone and anyone to dream up an activity based around the numbers 2.6 or 26 and make a donation to a chosen charity for completing the activity. There were no rules - except keep to social distancing and avoiding putting yourself or others in hospital.

So as a family group of various talents, interests and self-delusional abilities, this was game on! We all selected short, low key activities and pledged money to the local Food Bank. Up first was Daniel, aged 16, who had to be convinced that '26 kills on Call of Duty' was not in the spirit of the event. So, a reluctant 26 minutes' worth of cutting the garden lawn was negotiated. Dan, aged 22, opted for 26 press ups. Sarah, aged 19 also went for a fitness move, lifting our Maine Coon, Mo, 26 times off the floor. I do not expect 'cat squats' will be a new Olympic event any time soon. Diana went for a leisurely 26 minutes on the garden swing. Jess the cockerpoo ate 26 mini-bics from a puppy puzzle feeder, and I went for 26 football keepie-uppies. *Easy* - in my football glory days reaching over 100 was a literal walk in the park. All very straightforward. You would think.

Daniel's lawn-mowing skills left tufts of grass everywhere, and several border plants came to an untimely end. Dan delivered 24 press ups with relative ease, but over-stretched on number 25, before face-crashing into the grass on 26. Cat squats has left Mo traumatised, and he now refuses to come out from behind the compost heap. Sarah, a psychology student has taken this badly. Diana realised that non-stop swinging is for

10-year-olds high on sugar content and hated every second of it. It took me 31 attempts to reach 26 keepie-uppies and I felt humiliated by the whole experience. In my defence the ball I used was one Jess has ripped apart and can no longer be defined as 'round'...or a 'ball' really.

This morning's on-line church sermon had already warned of what happens when we start to rely on our own strengths, talents and gifts. In John's Gospel Chapter 21, Jesus and the disciples had just finished the fish meal on the beach. Then, three times Jesus asks Simon Peter 'do you love me?' and each time the disciple replies, 'Yes, Lord, you know that I love you'. Jesus knows the answer already, but here he is showing Peter the responsibility of real discipleship; ultimately for him 'to feed my sheep'.

In denying his Lord three times after Jesus' arrest in Jerusalem, Peter was falling back on the default button of sin, or *self*. Essentially, he was denying Christ and putting himself first, in effect relying on his own survival instincts. We do this all the time. *How can I do this in my own way? How can I use my own talents and strengths to get through this? I don't need anyone's help - got this one covered*. Often, we come unstuck, run into a cul-de-sac, or just simply overestimate our own ability. Sometimes by relying on self, we end up hurting others. Like Dan doing his press-ups, I have fallen on my face a thousand times, and consequently call on the Lord to reinstate me...again...and again. Today we raised some money for a good cause, which is great. It also reminded me that we are not quite as self-sufficient as we think we are. Thank God.

27th April: *The New Normal*

After recovering from Covid-19, Boris Johnson has returned to 10 Downing Street to lead the government once again. It will be interesting to see how this experience has changed the PM, both as a politician, and as a person. His deputies did an able job, but in this setting and context, it is good to have the political leader of the country back in the hot seat. I personally did not vote for Boris, but I have sought of missed his self-determined exuberance, ill-fitting suits, and unkempt hair. He returns to tackle questions the media have been seeking responses to, with the conflict between the health of the people and the health of the economy coming to a head. With other countries loosening the strings, the Conservative Cabinet have only managed to deflect rather than pacify the craving for concrete answers on when and how the UK will exit the lockdown. And we thought Brexit was a tangle of woes.

The phrase that has emerged as the exit strategy soundbite has been 'the new normal' - echoed again by Foreign Secretary Dominic Raab in today's live press gathering. But what is this 'new normal', and will we know when it arrives? It is all a bit guesswork, but the continuation of social distancing in shops, in offices and in factories may be the 'norm' for many months to come. The British art of queueing politely without fuss and drama will have to be put to the test. A new eating and drinking out in public arrangement could be enforced. Less tables, designated spaces in which to stand, and beer gardens may become commonplace. Schools? Possibly the centre of the first phase of any exit strategy; at least It is thought having nursery, infant and primary schools operating on restricted levels - only if to stop the nation's parents from going completely loop-fruit.

Back in front of my work laptop the MS Teams meeting this afternoon focused on life after lockdown for both teaching staff and the 2,500 students in their care. So far, as a college we had gone from little experience of remote learning to providing a decent stab at off-site engagement. Post lockdown, the cash strapped Further Education sector would need to dive deeply into what is known as *blended learning*, with the new normal moving us towards learning outside of the traditional classroom setting. Covid-19 has forced the hand of educators. The digital curriculum is here.

On a more sinister note, for other citizens of planet earth, the new normal could mean greater surveillance, less autonomy, and less freedom. Covid-19 may become an excuse for governments to curtail public liberty. There is evidence already that in China, the state authorities are putting in a range of measures to keep track of their citizens. An increasing use of QR codes to access homes and the workplace, the rolling out of facial recognition technology that can detect elevated temperatures in a crowd, and a new focus on the collection of mass personal data.

In our relatively blessed liberal democracy, there will be no such issues to content with. *He writes in hope*. What we *have* seen to date is a flood of kindness, sacrifice of self for others, indisputable financial generosity, and a concern for community. It would be a shame if this opportunity to create a new *better* normal in how we treat each other is not taken. What a great shame it would be if this sense of generous of spirit and unconditional love fades with the dissipation of this cruel coronavirus. A new normal in which we slow down, turn back to nature for reflection and solace, eat together at the family table, give up our own time for those more vulnerable, and put community before profit. That is a *new normal* to really look forward to, however surreal it may seem now.

29th April: *Birthday Wishes*

Two birthdays. Two different ends of the circle of life. Having recovered from coronavirus, and before he can get his feet well and truly back under his Downing Street desk, Boris Johnson becomes a father for a sixth time. With four grown up children in the bag from his first marriage, and a fifth child with another woman, Boris has had a baby boy with his fiancée Carried Symonds. No name yet, but looking at his other children's names, including Lara Lettuce, Theodore Apollo and Cassia Peaches, it's not going to be John, Michael, Mark or Simon. As if the man has not had his hands full lately. The positive story here is that Carrie (who also contracted Covid-19) and Boris Jnr are doing well.

At the other end of the age spectrum, is everyone's favourite fundraiser, Captain Tom Moore who is 100 years old tomorrow. The Second World War veteran has now raised over £29 million for the NHS by walking laps of his garden in Bedfordshire. He has received more than 125,000 cards from fans around the world, and from April 30th, all mail sent to Tom will be stamped with a special postmark in his honour.

Sitting healthily in between 0 and 100, my Dad celebrated his 87th birthday today. Thanks to the M&S gift delivery service, we sent Dad a VE Day Commemorative hamper of biscuits, chocolates, liquorice allsorts, topped off with two bottles of Spitfire Beer. My parents live in the shadow of Epsom Downs Racecourse and with Mum still receiving immunotherapy treatment at The Marsden Hospital, they have been under strict self-isolation. Unable to visit in person, I put together a failsafe action plan for myself and siblings to Zoom my parents and conduct our first ever family conference call.

My sister Lynne is still going into work every day at The Children's Trust in Tadworth. As an office manager, she describes herself as a 'backroom key worker' supporting the frontline carers. My brother Robert, a secondary school teacher, lives in Ashford Middlesex with his family. Knowing my Dad's limited IT skills, and my Mum's perchance for putting Dad under pressure, we had put this event off since lockdown. During the day I sent the Zoom meeting link via email to Dad, sister and brother. At 7.30 the three siblings appeared on screen as hoped for. No sign of Mum and Dad.

Mum called my mobile. 'Your Dad is having a few problems', she said. 'Aaah' I said, face grimacing into our laptop at the others. While Diana caught up with the clan with small talk, I tried to trouble shoot. 'It's right click Dad....can you paste into the browser?' Nope. 'You may need to download the App Dad'. Mum relayed instructions through her mobile phone. 'David, did you hear that? Try clicking again. They are waiting'. Sister Lynne's two young boys were now pulling faces at their end. 'No Dad, it's Microsoft...*not microwave*. Have you seen the Zoom icon yet?'. 'David, did you hear that one, Paul said have you found the Zoom icon jet?' Things were spiralling out of control. Computer had said *No* several times.

It was for the best that after a noisy rendition of Happy Birthday via Zoom through two loosely connected mobile phones, we called it a night. I will try again tomorrow with Dad - at his own pace. It was good though to catch up 'live' with Robert and Lynne to see how they were faring. The exercise had not all been in vain. I know he would have appreciated the attempt. Happy Birthday Dad.

30th April: *Living by Numbers*

As we move through a sixth week of lockdown in the UK, there is a sense things are coming to a head. Chief Boris is back taking the daily briefings, and there is more and more evidence at street level that the natives are getting restless. The long warm dry spell that made the lockdown more bearable has been replaced by cooler rainy weather across the British Isles. We are told that in terms of statistics, we have reached and even passed the peak of the virus. It seems every other country in mainland Europe has started to ease restrictions on movement, with key businesses and industry open for trade. Added to this, the liberal right wing in the United States are demanding their life back using street demonstrations to voice their frustrations. It is not surprising that this same frustration is building up here, but the Government is holding its nerve, following the latest scientific advice. Advice, including the use of face masks, that seems to be different to other scientific advice being given abroad. It comes down to how each government collates data and interprets the numbers. In particular, three pieces of data are being looked at by the UK's Coronavirus Response team.

Firstly, The R number - the number of people each infected person passes the disease on to. If R is kept below 1 the number of cases will not suddenly soar.

Secondly, the death rate is seen as significant. This is the number of deaths as a direct result from Covid-19, and the indirect number of deaths from the effect of shutting down society and different parts of the health service.

Thirdly, the actual number of cases of Covid-19, and the associated pattern and rate of expected decrease. In the last 24 hours, there has been an increase of 6,032 confirmed cases.

Comparisons with figures from other countries is also adding to the stress load for all. Without one common system used, like-for-like comparisons can be misleading. Under pressure, the government are now including the number of care home and community deaths for England and Wales to align with Scotland and other European nations. So, in one day, there has subsequently been a huge leap to 26,711. One of the government medical scientists has insisted that when the dust has settled, it is the *excess national death rate relative to the norm* which will eventually give us a more realistic comparison between countries. Only then will the finger pointing really start. What was it that Mark Twain famously said? *'There are lies, damn lies, and statistics'* a wisely depressing thought.

One of the books in the Bible I am least familiar with is the Book of Numbers. The fourth in the Old Testament, hence the fourth book of the Jewish Torah. This ancient scripture follows the Israel nation out of Egypt into the 'wilderness' (the Hebrew title for the book) as it seeks the Promised Land. The first chapters explain how Moses separated the people into 12 tribes at Mount Sinai, with the numbers for each tribe precisely stated in the text. So, they set off for Canaan with great expectation in their hearts. Yet things did not go as they hoped. Why did it take the Israelites nearly 40 years to transverse a relatively small area of desert, instead of the expected several days? Part of the way into their journey, the Israelites found themselves at the cross-roads, both geographically and spiritually. At a road intersection at Kadesh came Israel's crises of faith. The people rebelled against Moses and God upon hearing a report on the dangers of entering Canaan, delivered to them by 'ten faithless spies'. From that point in the journey they grumbled, complained and set their hearts against the Lord. As a result of their disobedience, the adult Israelites (except for Joshua and Caleb), were barred from entering the Promised Land for a generation.

Much like the Israelites in the wilderness, we are in danger of setting our hearts against God when things appear not to go as planned. I hope and pray that Covid-19 is not with us for forty years, but it is still tempting to call out to God for answers, and rebuke Him when the reply appears to be *silence*. Yet it is in these times of greatest despair and suffering that we need to turn towards Him in faith. Ironically, the book of Numbers is best known for five short lines of words; a benediction prayer based on

Chapter 6 verse 24-26. By reading it again, I am reminded that when we are wandering through the wilderness, if we ask in faith, God's voice can be heard loud and clear.

> "The LORD bless you and keep you;
> the LORD make his face shine upon you
> and be gracious to you;
> the LORD turn his face toward you
> and give you peace."

1st May: *Back in the USSR*

Friday night is quiz night. Dan's radio producer friend Will has been an 'Absolute' trooper in keeping this going for the past seven weeks. Using Google Hangouts, Will brings together over 20 teams - two quiz slots on the Friday and another on the Saturday. Donations to Love Works was the important purpose behind the fun. When I say 'fun', things were becoming a little bit stressful, as the Friday 8.30 quiz slot had become a very competitive two hours of mental gymnastics. Ten teams grappling for glory after spending another week virtually trapped in small flats, busy households and in some cases, self-isolation. It had all led to a very tight finish most weeks.

Last Friday *137 Covid Street* had taken the crown with a storming last round, pipping us by a point. Other teams like *Pam and the Demics* and The *PPE Hunters*, had recently strengthened their hands by bringing in extra players connected by other mobile devices. This was serious stuff. So we decided *The Flufighters* also required assistance in the form of Sarah's boyfriend Owen, a 23 year old accountant all the way from Essex. Owen's presence on his mobile had helped us previously to a couple of high finishes, but the number one spot had so far eluded us. So with Mo the Maine Coon perched in his usual spot on the piano, Diana (as scribe), Dan (music specialist), Sarah (food and drink guru) and myself (too much pressure to cover all other topics) settled down on the sofas. We were armed with the usual stockpile of soft drinks and sugary snacks.

The Picture round was the usual warm up, followed by General Knowledge and the incredibly hard 'Who said this?' round. So firstly, educated guesses ensued on the identity of famous characters cunningly disguised with Will's head digitally supplanted on their necks. In round Two, knowing the writer of Les Miserable and the names of David and Victoria Beckham's four children gave us a solid score. However, the 'Who said this? round caused the usual grief. If the quotes were not from Churchill, Gandhi, Shakespeare or the Dali Lama, then why would you know or care what Dani Dyer, Gemma Collins or Michael Gove has said! Luckily, the Music round clawed us back into contention. I did not feel that proud however, knowing D-Ream had once sung a track called 'Things can only get better'.

After the drinks break, we found ourselves off the pace, with The *PPE Hunters* taking a strong lead. However, the Sport round was kind to us. 'Pickle' was the name of the dog who found the Jules Rimet Trophy in 1966, and we scored maximum points for the seven FA Cup winners since 2006. Round Six - TV and Movies. Step forward Owen who it seems has watched every film and America drama and state-side comedy since the age of three. He smashed the big nine-pointer for instance, naming all of the characters who made up The Fellowship of the Ring.

The question stumping every team? Postman Pat's surname! High- brow stuff indeed.

Round Seven - Geography. We smashed this one. Being a travel and tourism lecturer for many years helped, and Owen somehow knew the six countries which border Iraq. Moving into the final round, we had edged a point in front. After last week, the nerves were tangible, and beginning to fray. More Pringles and Morrison's own brand popcorn were quickly consumed, and some of us went far too hard on the white grape Shloer.

The History Round. Not our favourite. Also finishing strongly, the *NHS Heroes* had a history graduate in their team. Cheats! We struggled on the exact years needed for two questions, and *The Flufighters* were left flummoxed on which Prime Minister did what in the C20th. I pulled out the inventor of the bouncing bomb from the recesses of my memory bank, and we pulled the *country which first had the women's vote* out the educated-guess bag.

But it all came down to the wire, with the last question of the evening worth 15 points. '*In 1991, the dissolution of the USSR led to 15 countries gaining political independence. Name them.*' Thanks to Owen, whose knowledge of Eastern European countries (which always struggle in the

European Championship qualifying groups) was solid, and we had a good stab at it. We did not get Kyrgyzstan nor Tajikistan, but we named the other 13. But was it enough?

The tension was unbearable when Will read out the final scores. *We did it, by one point!* Howls of joy and various trampoline moves on sofas from the Banthorpe household was greeted by a generous clap from our competitors. The real winners though were those participants in self-isolation who really enjoy and value this time to communicate with others; and the charity, Love Works of course. Well done Will, another great event to lift the spirits. The pressure was now off, and next Friday we could focus on 'the taking part' rather than the 'winning'. Shame on us.

3rd May: *Expectant Prayer*

Thank goodness for the modern tech-miracles of Zoom, MS Teams, Google Hangout and Facebook during the coronavirus lockdown. Either for leisure activities or for fulfilling work functions these e-tools have been the saviours of human interconnectivity. Yet even in this modern age of digital advancement, they are not perfect. The blips, gremlins and glitches we have experienced over the past seven weeks are testament to this, and it has made me appreciate the accessibility and ease we have in talking to God. Could you imagine during our prayers, a little blue circle suddenly appearing in our minds to indicate buffering or a weak connection? *Sorry, God cannot hear you right now, you're on mute!*

Most mornings I wake up and reach for my iPhone to read Verse of the Day, written by Phil Ware, an American Pastor who is also the President and editor of Heartlight on-line devotionals. Today's verse is from Psalm 5:3,

>*In the morning, O Lord you hear my voice; in the morning I lay my requests before you and wait in expectation*

In his short exposition, Phil Ware suggests prayer is more than just making requests, offering praise, giving thanks and the intercession for others. He says, *it is expecting that God wants us there*. Prayer therefore, is our expectation that God firstly hears us, and then will respond to our prayers. Prayer, Phil adds, *is eagerly expecting God will meet us in our prayer time and do what is best for us and those we love.* But that is not all. Prayer is completely free of charge, totally accessible 24/7 and you do not need a Degree in Theology to be able to use this hotline to heaven. There are no boundaries, no pre-conditions and Jesus taught us what to say and how to say it. In fact, the only ingredient we bring to the table is *faith*. It does not have to be much, and usually isn't! But the message above is clear. *Lay your requests before Him, and wait in expectation*. It seems that during this period of life uncertainty, more and more people are doing just that.

The Christian charity Tearfund carried out a poll of over 2,000 adults between 24th and 27th April. 5% of respondents said they have started to pray during the lockdown, having not prayed before. 5% had watched or listened to a religious service, having never attended a church service before. 26% said they were praying for themselves and others at this time when only 6% of the British public attend church on a regular basis. Not only that, more young people (aged 18-24) in the survey gave a more positive response than the over 55s. Tearfund's Dr Ruth Valerio responded to the survey findings;

'It is encouraging to see the number of people in the UK praying during such a challenging time. Our experience at Tearfund is that prayer and practical action go hand-in-hand and are both crucial ways of responding.'

I have found the most effective prayer is spontaneous, natural and focuses on seeking the presence of a God who has always been there for me. I am still learning that the expectation is not that He will respond immediately, abiding to my every request; but it is the expectation that He does hear. He does care for me, and He does want what is best for me and those I love. That is the power of tech-free expectant prayer.

4th May: *(Be with You)*

Not so long ago, in a galaxy not so far away….

It was a dark time for the planet called Earth.
In the absence of faith, hope and charity,
A phantom menace swept through the lands.
Sent by the evil empire of hate and destruction,
This silent weapon struck down young and old alike.
A band of masked resistance fighters stood firm,
Tending those left sick by the rising tyranny;
While many faced lockdown in their own homes
As they waited for a spark of new hope.
So, the believers prayed for a sign from beyond the stars,
As they waited for the return of the one true light.
For this light shines in the darkness,
And the darkness can never extinguish it.

6th May: *Cat's Eyes*

They call me Mo. When they get excited and demand my attention it is Mo-Mo. The old auntie cat who lived with me has gone - I think she was sick. I could smell it on her. I do not feel I need to stay up the stairs anymore, for she is safe now. So now every day I come down the stairs. It reminds me of other friends I also lived with. There was a big-pawed creature with kind eyes. They liked her a lot. I also remember another one who looked more like me - she used to play with me in the garden. We were close. Family perhaps. To be honest, it is all a bit of a blur. But I have instinct. I sense when things are good, and not so good. Even with my new down the stairs courage, I sense something is not quite right.

It could be the presence of that other bouncy creature with the loud snappy noise. I try to ignore her, but she wants to play with me. I say play, more like chase. She is always very excitable and...very, very bouncy. Sometimes she looks at me saying 'what are you?' She will get used to me, in time. I am trying very hard to live with her. They like her a lot too. So, I will try for them.

I sense a difference in what *they* do. They are always here for me. This is not the same as before when they were not always here. I know what to do every day to get what I need. When the light appears, I leave my basket and try to wake up the one they call Paul Dad. He lies on his back and makes loud grunting noises, a bit like the bouncy creature. But worse! To get him out of his padded basket I scratch on wood. If that does not work, I make whining noises. We Maine Coons do not 'meoow' as the other ones do. We whine, chirp and chatter. If that does not work, I have a new routine. The old auntie taught me this as she grew weaker. I go into the space they call *bathroom* and climb into a large white tub thing. I then do my daily lumps. And wait. This usually works, the Paul Dad eventually gets up and I know it is the start of the day.

He feeds me down the stairs, then he gets the bouncy fur-ball up next. He feeds me first though. Chew on that fur-ball!

After *num-nums* - this is the only sound I understand apart from *Mo* - I come back up the stairs and curl up in my basket again. Down the stairs I can hear lots of their voices all day. It used to be quiet. The noises I hear the most are 'Jess, good girl', 'Jess, come here', 'Jess biscuit' and very often "Jessica, what have you done?'. When bouncy has been put away in her cage after late num-nums, I then come down the stairs and sit quietly with them. This is the time I like the best. I get lots of cuddles and watch the moving picture with them for hours. My favourite moving picture is called *Paw O'Gravy loves Trogs*. There are lots of noisy bouncy fur-balls in cages so they cannot chase us Maine Coons. I Like that one.

Lots of change for Mo. Furry friends disappearing. Lots of *them* appearing all at once. But I feel more important now, being the only creature living here that looks like me. I have all I need. They give me cuddles and lots of num-nums. I sleep in my basket for hours. I no longer have to go down the stairs to do my daily lumps. Life is good for me.

7th May: *You'll Never Walk Alone*

There has been a lot of reference to 'heroes' during this pandemic. Certainly, in modern times the term has been overused and therefore often undervalued. Tonight, we clapped again for the carers, joining in with an ever growing crescendo from neighbours down both sides of the road.

Our frontline workers *are* heroes in the true meaning of the term. Sacrificing self for the greater good is a noble characteristic and I wonder if I was a nurse, a care home worker or a paramedic would I wear that same trait as well? I asked Diana who her hero was. I was expecting her to say her late father who she was really close to, but she reminded me that the team of surgeon's who operated on her four years ago were her choice. Indeed, after she had recuperated from the nine-hour Diep Flap surgery, she sent them a thank you card calling them her 'heroes'. 'They treated me with such dignity and respect that day, it helped me to cope, she said. 'I'll never forget that.'

Growing up, like so many like-minded pre-teen dreamers around the world, my heroes were initially found in the pages of comic books. My collection of Spiderman comics from the 1970s and the accompanying Spidey Paraphernalia that sits on the shelves of my unofficial mancave are among my most favoured worldly possessions. I *so* wanted to have a special power at the age of ten. It was not whether this would happen or not, it was just a matter of fact that one day I would be bitten by a radioactive insect or fall into a vat of super jelly. Of course, a super-power never came, although recently I have discovered I may have acquired one. I now have an advanced sense of smell, waking up from the deepest of sleeps when Mo's bath routine hits my nostrils! It was a super-power I could do without.

The underground artist Banksy has just poured very cold water over my web-slinging boyhood hero. His latest masterpiece, left in the lobby of Southampton General Hospital overnight, depicts a young boy playing with a nurse doll in a cape. Toy figures of Spiderman and Superman are left discarded in a bin next to him, looking rather sorry for themselves.

The nation has another hero, Captain Tom Moore. Having completed his 100 garden laps and then celebrating his 100th birthday, the latest total raised through his Just Giving page stood at well over £32 million. Tom suffers from arthritis, skin cancer and er....is 100 years old. He even has a number one record under his belt now, after recording 'You'll never walk alone' with everyone's favourite baritone, Michael Ball. A very interesting song - not written by Gerry and the Pacemakers in 1963 as many believe - but written by Rodgers and Hammerstein for the musical Carousel in 1945. I listened to the original earlier; quite a stage barnstormer and not one Liverpool supporter chanting in the background. The lyrics are incredibly moving, and mirror both the endeavours of Captain Tom and the sentiment of togetherness during this pandemic. Diana's favourite piece of writing is the Christian poem, 'Footprints' which also considers the need for help in the darkest times of life. As a tribute to Captain Tom, my wife (who is my real hero), and all those who are putting themselves in the firing line for the sake of others on a daily basis, here is my combined take on these lovely words.

> You walked with me through the dreams of my life
> Double footprints carved in sands of time,
> I held to the hope of forever gold skies
> Where songs of the lark soar so high.
>
> Yet in the darkest of days I felt lonely with fear,
> Tossed and blown by the wind and the rain,
> So I question why when I needed you most,
> You left me alone to deal with my pain?
>
> 'My child' said a voice, 'During those long days of hurt,
> When you believed you were lost and alone,
> You see where two sets of prints become one,

That was when I carried you back home.'
So walk on, walk on
With hope in your heart
Walk towards the eternal goal
Walk on walk on
With faith in your heart
And you'll never walk alone.

8th May: *VE Day*

We woke early Tuesday, filled with excitement and anticipation for the day ahead. A quick face scrub followed by jam on toast was washed down by a small glass of milk. I put on my favourite air force blue lumber jacket. Uncle Ted had given me another stripe he didn't want, and mum sowed it onto the left sleeve. I was now a sergeant major at the age of twelve! My dad smiled at me with pride from his lounge chair, squinting to see the three white chevrons. Mustard gas had taken away most of his sight in the Great War, and mum says he has never been the same man since. My parents won't be coming with me today, Uncle Alec popped round yesterday to say London would be very crowded. For obvious reasons my dad doesn't like crowds, and mum will stay at home with him. Auntie Edie, who lives upstairs, and Auntie Win, who lives in the next street, will take me to the celebrations.

At ten o'clock, we made the short walk to Upton Park station to catch the underground. The carriage was full, bursting with suited gentleman in caps, ladies in colourful dresses, with a few young men dressed in full army uniform smoking merrily, standing at one end. Auntie Win sat with me while Auntie Edie, who looks after me as if I were her own, stood over us like a hen protecting her chicks. I was pleased when we reached Charring Cross, the carriage smoke had started to irritate, and a foul sweaty smell was coming from the man sitting to my right. The fresh air when we reached the surface was a joy. Almost immediately songs filled the open sky. The melodies coming from a wave of people spread across Charing Cross Road, a thousand expectant feet moving slowly in unison. The two Aunties gripped a hand each as we became caught up in the mass of bodies. All I could see were the backs of those in front of me, the pace slowing significantly as we passed The Epitaph down Whitehall. I could just see the top of Nelson's Column on the skyline and took a deep breath.

It seemed ages before we finally reached the open arena of Trafalgar Square. To my left a group of soldiers formed a long conga, lined with young breezy skirts and shirts, and older Londoners shouted out the words to *Pack up Your Troubles*. Ahead of me the crowd seemed a hundred deep leading up to the famous four lions. Auntie Win pointed out one soldier who had shimmied twenty feet up a lamp post, clinging to the top in a crab position. The noise was deafening, it was midday and the sun finally peeked out from a bank of clouds to brighten the scene with shafts of light.

The war in Europe was over Winston said yesterday, and for the first time I believed it. No more long nights in the underground, no more lying awake in my own bed listening out for the death whine of unannounced V1 rockets. I was filled with a great wave of relief. It would be back to school again tomorrow, and I could not wait to tell my friends that I was *here,* in Trafalgar, witnessing this moment. The impromptu singalongs, a canopy of Union Jacks thrust in the air, and the sight of couples dancing in fountains would stay with me forever. 'Come on David, let's be making our way back' smiled Auntie Edie, 'we can still get home in time to listen to the Prime Minister on the radio.' And that is exactly what we did.

It is now 75 years since Britain and its allies accepted the unconditional surrender of Nazi Germany. This special Bank Holiday Friday was meant to be cram packed with parades and street parties, trestle tables topped with cucumber sandwiches and scones, craft beer flowing from pint glasses, and children wrapped in bunting, running freely from house to house. Covid-19 had put a huge spanner in the works and compromise was the order of the day. After the two-minute silence at eleven, watching a variety of TV specials, and re-living Churchill's speech at three, we set up in the front garden. Organised by our Neighbourhood Watch co-ordinator, most of the road appeared for drinks and nibbles. Social distancing style. We enjoyed Pimm's, hotdogs and the best M&S Victoria sponge money can buy. For the first time in weeks, live conversations replaced the screen chats, and human interaction flowed like milk and honey. The younger children used the middle of the road as a scooter track, and the dogs greeted each other at the end of extended leads. As the sun faded, we treated ourselves to pizza delivery, and to top it all, we won the Friday quiz for the second week running. In a lockdown context, it was a pretty good day.

Earlier in the week my parents solved their Zoom issues and we all made visual contact. Dad's eyes lit up as we connected. Mum even let him speak. Today I phoned him back. 'So what do you remember about VE Day, Dad?' I asked. 'Oh not much, I was only a boy at the time', he replied. 'Take your time'. I said, 'Just talk me through your day... I'll jot a few notes down'. After a short pause, he started to talk, and I could hear the sense of history in his voice.

'We woke early on Tuesday with excitement and anticipation for the day ahead........'

10th May: *The Big Exit Plan*

In this morning's on-line church service, Senior Pastor Graham took his sermon from the first chapter of the Book of Acts. The theme of this new series of sermons is *Transformed* and focuses on the early church in Jerusalem, when the message of Jesus' life, death and resurrection is taken by his followers to both the Jews and the Gentiles. Jesus had appeared to hundreds of people over a total of forty days and now it was time for his Ascension. It was Diana who brought the reading (verses 1-11) to the on-screen congregation, which now numbered over a hundred each Sunday. I had filmed her in the snug (or my unofficial mancave) on Thursday using my iPhone in only two takes. She spoke well, but the finished clip was clearly not directed by Spielberg or produced by the Russo brothers.

The Book of Acts was written by Doctor Luke, the one who brought us the third Gospel. A man who took down notes meticulously, an eye for observational detail, and someone who chose his words carefully. The various English translations of the Bible not always doing this last point justice. Essentially if Luke was a first Century blogger, the 'likes' would now be in the tens of millions! In the passage Jesus explains to his disciples and other close followers what will happen next. He was leaving them in human form and knew they were to face many trials and challenges. But God had a *Jesus exit plan!* Soon the next phase of salvation would be put into action through the coming of the Holy Spirit, who would guide and empower the disciples as they ventured out into the world to bear witness to all they had seen and heard.

'But you will receive power when the Holy Spirit comes on you;
and you will be my witnesses in Jerusalem, and in all Judea and Samaria, and to the ends of the earth' (v8)

One of my favourite James Bond characters is Q, the weapons expert originally played by the late Desmond Llewelyn. In The World Is Not Enough (1999) Llewelyn, in his final appearance in the franchise, gives Bond, played by Pierce Bronson words of advice.

Q: 'I've always tried to teach you two things: First, never let them see you bleed.'
Bond: 'And the second?'
Q: 'Always have an escape plan."

As the nation sat down to listen to a special broadcast from the Prime Minister at seven O'clock these words resonated in my head. The government led by Boris Johnson had for several days indicated that the next phase of the fight against coronavirus in the UK had arrived. We all wanted to know what the exit strategy, or the carefully staged escape plan might be. Boris had to find the balance between protecting our health and bringing us out of lockdown so the economy could start to recover. We listened intently to his strong words of pride induced rhetoric, interspersed by hand waving and notable table thumping. We had *all done very well*, and a series of graphs seemed to suggest the numbers were right to ease things a bit. The problem started when the new slogan was announced: *Stay alert, Control the Virus, Save Lives.*

Stay alert? What does that mean exactly? What made matters worse was the fact that Scottish, Welsh, and Northern Irish ministers had stuck to the old slogan, *Stay at Home.*

Boris continued: if you can still work from home, do so, but if you can't then you can go back to work tomorrow - but try not to use public transport, which the key workers are using; perhaps walk or cycle instead. At work, you must social distance, (but employers have not had the full guidance on this yet); oh, and you can meet up with others, but on a 1:1 basis. *Was that just family members or friends too?* Not clear. Boris went on: and another thing, you can go out as far as you want and for as much as you want. *Can someone in Bristol travel to Wales for a day out, then?* Dan thought out aloud. Boris again: and all this is conditional, if it does not work, then we go back to more stringent measures. Step two - Primary schools could be opening their doors again in June; step three - certain hospitality and catering outlets can open in July... But it is all conditional. Another hand wave....table thump...and *we can all do this together.* Hard stare into the camera. Goodbye.

By the end of the speech we were all mentally scrambled. It was not long before the satirists got to work - notably a 20 second You Tube post from Matt Lucas spoofing Boris went viral. Even Philip Schofield lost his rag live on *This Morning* twelve hours later. New Labour Leader Sir Keir Starmer didn't have to work too hard to find holes in this government exit strategy. Apparently, the detail behind the confusing message is published in a 50-page manual.

This was the first time I had really lost my rag too. The strategy seemed to be based on political spin rather than a response to hard scientific research. Less a clear path to lockdown easing, more an indiscernible Rubik Cube of words. Another reminder how human we are. God's exit plan for Jesus still holds good after 2,000 years. Probably unfair to compare the present UK Government with the Holy Spirit. Thank God. Again.

12th May: *Lady of the Lamp*

For the past two days England has been reeling from the confusion caused by Boris' speech. The 'go back to work' call led to a noticeable increase in the use of public transport on Monday, only for the government message to change to 'go back to work if you need to this Wednesday', but 'only if social distancing can be maintained in the workplace'. All of a sudden, the wearing of masks in tight public spaces is endorsed after weeks of scientific evidence suggesting they only provide negligible protection. Furthermore, meeting up with one other person you do not live with is now acceptable, but please keep the two metres apart rule. Golf and tennis are also allowed. Has Monty Python returned?

Charged by...well just about everyone...with sliding the country to into a state of bewilderment, Boris fought back by saying he is relying on the *Great British Common Sense* - whatever that is? I assume by *common sense* he is talking about how we make the right decisions based on previous life experience? Given X, then Y is the most appropriate response etc. *If I put my finger in this light socket, it may hurt...so I won't.* Got it. Just that not many of us have experienced life during a world pandemic before. There is nothing 'common' about it. Which is why we have been told to act and behave according to the best expert advice going. *Until now apparently.* Now we just have to make it up as we go along, based on gut feeling and...*uncommon sense*.

The other worrying aspect of the past couple of days is the re-emergence of coronavirus growth spikes in countries that had already eased their lockdowns. Germany, who had seen off Covid-19 with almost annoying efficiency, has seen a rise in infections, and France, Italy and Spain are still grappling with new hot spots of contagion as a result of lockdown easing. Further abroad, South Korea is declaring new outbreaks, and what can you say about Trump's USA? Several states which are now restarting their economies have infection rates that are still rising. The UK was now attempting at jump-starting its economy as the death toll neared 40,000. Yes, daily infection rates and hospital admissions had passed their peaks, but something did not feel right about pushing the boat back out to sea when storm clouds still gathered overhead.

On a brighter note, today is International Nurses Day (IND), and this coincides with the bi-century anniversary of the birth of the founder of modern nursing. This is not a random coincidence, as in 1972, May 12th was chosen as the date to celebrate IND: Florence Nightingale's birthday. The poignancy of this day has never been greater. Stories of the excellent professionalism and personal care given by our nurses to those suffering and recovering from Covid-19 are told every day. To his credit, Boris led the plaudits to Florence with these words on his Twitter page;

"She revolutionised Victorian healthcare, establishing principles that stand to this day. She changed and shaped the very perception of what a nurse is, what a nurse should be, transforming the job into what she called 'the finest of fine arts'.

I am going to leave the final say to the Dean of Westminster Abbey who said this prayer as a mark of respect to the 'Lady of the Lamp' in a special service commemorating her life in 2018. The reference to *the father of lights* is inspired by verse 17 from the first chapter of the book of James.

O God the father of lights, from you comes every good and perfect gift:
we thank you for Florence Nightingale and for her vision, courage, and
compassion, of which this Lamp is the undying symbol. Kindle our hearts,
we pray, by the fire of your Holy Spirit, so that we may shine for you in
the darkness of human suffering and sorrow;
through him who is light of the world, our Saviour Jesus Christ.
Amen

14th May: *Fairies and Imps*

T'was a morning in lockdown, and all through the house,
Not a sound could be heard, not from keyboard, nor mouse.
Two slippers awoke from their Covid nightmares,
And a fairy called Spick tiptoed quietly downstairs.

Firstly, he fed the cat biscuits and meat,
Then tidied the kitchen back to hygienic neat.
The dishwasher emptied, then all put away,
The kettle switched on; the first tea of the day.

Next out comes puppy from her sleep-easy crate,
Straight to the garden before it's too late!
Business all done, bowl filled to the brim.
Puppy wags gratefully for this routine with *him*.

Spick sprinkles fairy dust to make puppy stay,
Safe in the kitchen, out of harm's way,
Then back up the stairs with hot tea and warm toast
To the fairy called Span whom he loves the most.

Quick breakfast consumed, Fairy Span takes a shower,
Leaving her smelling like her favourite flower.
Then she dresses in rainbows and floats down the stairs,
She smiles at her home, saying blessings and prayers.

Span next greets the puppy with a kiss and a hug,
On goes the harness with a pull and a tug.
After her walkies, pup's back sound asleep
So out comes the broom; there's a hallway to sweep.

With a scrub and a rub, toilets now spotless and clean,
More fairy magic leaves the carpets pristine.
Then the two fairies dine on coffee and cake,
And wait for the Imps to finally awake!

The clock strikes at noon, the Imps crawl out of bed,
Eyes wide as saucers, hands rubbing their heads.
They walk like three zombies, but still find the fridge,
A small raiding party eating all they can binge.

Next back to their rooms to catch up with friends,
Texting peer Imps who live where the world ends.
Staring at screens until hunger comes back,
Then off to the kitchen to find *the* perfect snack.

The pattern repeats until the food has all gone.
The satisfied Imps say 'au revoir, so long',
Except here comes the clothes that smell of the week,
Dealing with 'smalls' is not for the meek!

At the end of the day, our two fairies look drained,
Yet the three little Imps are happily less strained!
But tired Spick and Span really don't mind,
For they know one day Imps will be adults.......
for a very long time

15th May: *Exposing the Divide*

The Covid -19 pandemic is exposing some of the divisions and inequalities that exist in society. This week it was confirmed that black men and women are nearly twice as likely to die with coronavirus as white people in England and Wales. Public Health England has already started a scientific review into the impact of the disease on frontline workers from ethnic minorities. Early findings indicate inequality in death rates persist even after age, location, deprivation, and prior poor health have been taken into account. Those from Indian, Bangladeshi, and Pakistani communities also have a higher risk of dying. Additional evidence has noted that a third of all those who have become critically ill from the virus are from BAME backgrounds.

One possible explanation for the statistics is that more people from BAME communities have underlying health conditions. Black people for instance are more likely to be overweight than white, while both Asian and black populations are more susceptible to the risk of diabetes and heart disease. Other indicators looked at in the research include social deprivation, larger over-crowded households and the *occupation factor*. BAME individuals are more likely to be on the NHS front line such as nurses, doctors and care workers at a disproportionate rate compared to the overall population average. Sadly, to support this research, many BAME workers have come forward since the start of the pandemic to give examples of discrimination in the workplace, with accusations of overt racism. Some testify to seeing colleagues, nurses and doctors selected for more dangerous duties in hospitals, while others point to the low level of BAME managers in the NHS despite the larger ratio of ethnic workers.

As well as the concern over racial prejudice, wider issues related to inequality are also being exposed. In her article published in the Guardian last month, Frances Ryan calls it the *hidden coronavirus crises*. She highlights the social fallout of lockdown. Women unable to escape abusive partners, vulnerable children cut off from social workers, low income families skipping meals due to reduced wages, high food bills and a lagging social security system. Food banks have never been busier. Other charities, the pillars of our wonderful voluntary sector, struggle to raise funds, or have ceased operations altogether. When you add it all up, Frances Ryan writes, *'society's least privileged are being hit hardest'*. I have not even mentioned the impact on mental health - *see my 18th May blog entry.*

Clearly, whatever your religious or political beliefs may be, we are *not all born equal,* as natural differences in birthplace, talent, intelligence, financial inheritance etc are part of human existence. The fact is we all have different starting points. So what does the Bible say about *inequality*? An initial reference source may be the American Declaration of Independence which declares, *we are all created equal*. The Bible endorses this subtle distinction. In God's eyes we are all equal in his sight. We all have the same value and worth. For God, it is never about race, but simply about grace. Every one of us can be a child of God, receiving the full inheritance of His kingdom.

If this is the case, then how should we respond to our fellow humankind? Looking to the One who humbled Himself to save me from my own failings never disappoints as a fundamental starting point. Jesus, who left the glory of heaven to die for us in such humiliating circumstances...'did not consider equality with God something to be used to his own advantage; rather he made himself nothing by taking the very nature of a servant' (Philippians 2 v 6). If the Son of God can wholly submit to others in love, then who are we not to do the same?

In response to the question, *which are the two greatest commandments?',* Jesus basically tells us there are only two! The greatest of which is;

'You shall love the Lord your God with all your heart and with all your heart and with all your strength' (Mark 12 v 30)

The evangelist Jack Wellman writes that this is the *vertical commandment,* relating to our relationship with God. Then Jesus gives the second, which Wellman describes as the *horizontal commandment,* and this deals with our relationship with others;

'You shall love your neighbour as yourself' (Mark 12 v 31)

A useful image to remember this by is *the cross*. The vertical beam intersecting a connected horizontal beam.

In God's creation there may be inequality but there is not hierarchy. The lockdown has opened up opportunities for selfless giving, but it is a challenge to us all to go much further, by treating all without prejudice and without the usual tempting conditions attached. In his letter to Ephesians, the apostle Paul sums this up well when he writes, 'submit to one another out of reverence for Christ' (5 v 21). Our response? Jesus told us to be the Good Samaritan to everyone, all the time. In doing so we are following the second greatest commandment of God.

16th May: *To Bee or Not to Bee*

Diana asked me the other day what was the thing I missed the most since lockdown. For her, it was just being with others. In particular, she was missing her church friends. Before I could give my response, she pointed at me like I had just eaten the dog. 'Ha! I know exactly what you are going to say', she said. Without moving my lips, Diana kept speaking for me, grinning with a devious twinkle in her eye, 'It's *football* isn't it? I knew it. I knew it. What does that say about you then?'

I shrugged. 'Maybe it is, maybe it isn't?' I grinned back. Married for two years and she had me sussed. Of course, she was on the right lines. I did miss the football, the hopes and disappointments, and the peer banter that goes with it.

In the absence of all things sport on the TV I have been lured into watching programmes that in normal circumstances I would avoid like the...er...you know what. When we first got married, Diana cast a cunning spell on me which seduced me into watching Springwatch, Countryfile, Gardener's World and wait for it...Antiques Roadshow. Yes, Sunday evenings flew by with the adrenalin rush you would expect from such edge of the seat viewing. Then, before I had a chance to recover my sanity, it was The Repair Shop - which I have to say has become a must watch; and creeping up on me unawares, For The Love of Dogs has got me weeping for more weekly Paul O'Grady canine magic.

As if that was not compromise enough (in return I can watch two football matches a week- I may need to re-negotiate this) Diana has taken complete advantage of escalating lockdown fatigue. For the past four weeks I have been pinned to the sofa glued to….. *The Great British Sewing Bee*. Seriously, this is brainwashing and mind control that the Russians would have been proud of in the Cold War. From the makers of The Great British Bake Off (Yep, I now love Sandi Toskvig), here is the fifth series of this sewing competition on Auntie Beeb. The 'Bee' in the title refers not to a Buzzing Thing (thanks Baldrick), but mirrors the Spelling Bee children's competition concept. 'Bee' referring to a social gathering of like-minded people carrying out communal work, often under pressure. Sewing. Right. A real pressure cooker of activity. There is no way this fifty something alpha male is going *to get into* that!

Four weeks into the competition. Three competitors down. It is *sports and leisure wear* week. The opening round - rugby shirts. This is all about getting the *placket* right, for the stitching must be strong enough to withstand the wear and tear. Round two - *transformation*: turning cagoules into children's onesies. I totally agreed with the judge's verdict. The winning garment matched glorious design with total practicality. That was followed by deciding Round three - *ladies tennis dresses*. This went down to the wire, but I confidently picked the winner, whose pattern combined tradition with modern fabrics. Get a load of that back stitching. Superb.

More important than my easy to please attitude, the programme has given Diana a real lift. A keen machinist, she has been offered the chance to make scrubs for NHS workers. Quite an honour, and commitment.

'I'm not sure? I haven't sewed complex patterns for ages. What do you think, Paul? Shall I? Perhaps not, my mum's old machine is a bit temperamental. I'd love to contribute. Shall I? Oh, I don't know'

Two days after her Hamlet soliloquy, a parcel arrived for Diana. *It's here!* The exact sewing machine used on TGBSB. We decided that this was a once in a lifetime opportunity. For lockdown I had purchased a ukulele to while away the hours, and Diana now has her own pass time investment. The scrubs material arrived already cut from pattern, and before you could say *Esme Young* (the original Edna Mode of course) you could hear the Janone 725s purring away in the kitchen. By 9 pm, the scrubs outfit was taking shape. Well, done Diana, so proud. Although the pocket lines needed squaring before you pinned.

17th May: *Virtual Reality*

Suffering from sport withdrawal syndrome (pretty sure that is an official term) I began surfing through the Freeview sports channels looking for a quick fix. At the moment I would watch *anything* that was slightly competitive and based on a loose collection of agreed rules. Give me deep sea fishing, tandem rock climbing, international marbles, even Australian (no)rules football. *Anything*. flicking past the obvious repeats of yesteryear, I found Formula 1 motor racing. Now I am not a huge fan of motor sport, and to be honest, I am totally out of touch with the cars and drivers. I continued to watch the cars scream around tight corners with accompanying commentary in the background. Then to my surprise small boxes with faces appeared at the bottom of the screen. Names of former and current drivers were listed too with statistics about the race. I then realised to my embarrassment that this was not real Formula 1 racing, but an e-Sport! I had been duped by high tech gaming. This was one of the many versions of e-Sports now being played around the world. Last year I tuned into a PlayStation FIFA competition to view seated competitors in complex headsets procrastinating with themselves and their virtual players. My son Daniel apparently is a regular voyeur of this form of gaming and let me know in no uncertain terms that this was *the sport of today...big business...players earning megabucks.*

So back to reality. The big sports story of the weekend - football is back! Football is *coming home*. Well, not exactly; the German Bundesliga is back, on our screens; Germany the first nation to allow its top division to complete the domestic season. Each match being played behind closed doors, yet aired live across Europe, was for the football fan the shot in the arm the doctor ordered. This afternoon Dan and myself watched Union Berlin v Bayern Munich. To add a little atmosphere, we played 'crowd noises and chants' on a laptop (Diana's face was priceless) and sat back to enjoy the game. It was very surreal. You could hear the thud of the ball every time it was kicked, hear every word uttered on the pitch - all the classics were there (and mostly in English!), *'you got* time'...'man on'...'box it'...and the unforgettable, ' idiot, *warum hast du den Ball nicht übergeben?*'

When a goal was scored, hugging and other bromance rituals were replaced by quick 'elbow touching' and 'player to player clapping'. When a player was injured, no-one would go up to him, standing over and looking concerned. Now everyone kept their distance while the poor player writhed around in agony. Which all seems a bit bonkers in a game which included tight marking, full body contact, and several clashes of heads. The substitutes looked on from the stands, sitting several seats apart and wearing club coloured face masks. Needless to say, the match had no atmosphere and Bayern won by two weirdly celebrated goals to nil. It all felt a bit virtual, like watching a FIFA on-line match. Realistic, yet not quite real.

In this morning's sermon on Zoom the same surreal experience was being had by bystanders in the passage from Acts Chapter 2. What they were witnessing did not quite add up. In the centre of Jerusalem they saw the early disciples and followers of Jesus acting really strange, speaking in many languages unknown to them, and behaving as if drunk. Seeing the bewilderment on the faces of the gathering crowd, Peter addressed them to explain what was happening;

> These people are not drunk, as you suppose. It's only nine in the morning!
> No, this is what was spoken by the prophet Joel:
> 'In the last days, God says,
> I will pour out my spirit on all people,
> Your sons and daughters will prophesy,
> Your young men will see visions,
> Your old men will dream dreams'

Can you imagine the scene on this Jewish day of Pentecost? The eyes do not lie, but the mind makes no sense of what is seen. The crowd were witnessing the power of God's Holy Spirit right before them, equipping the disciples with the supernatural means to go to the ends of the Earth to spread the Good News. This was the birth of the church built on the testimony that Jesus Christ is the living messiah of all humankind. This is virtual reality on a universal scale. In fact, my digital native son Daniel explained to me how virtual reality differs from *augmented reality*. VR immerses us in a fully artificial digital world, where nothing is as it seems. However, AR overlays virtual objects on the real-world so we can interact with it. Through the receiving of His Spirit, God wants us to know him in a deeper way, but this should not divorce us from the real world.

One of the criticisms I hear about Christians - *'oh, their heads are in the clouds, they don't know what it's like in the real world'* - is sometimes not too far from the truth. God wants us to be fully with Him, but have our feet firmly set in the world. Only then can we effectively *augment* His love to others. In the fast-moving world of virtual inter-connectivity, it is surely more important than ever to show God's human face in person.

18th May: *Kindness*

Today begins Mental Health Awareness Week in the UK organised by The Mental Health Foundation. The theme of the week is *kindness*, which fits in well with the current context. Most of us try to be 'kind' in different ways but actually we are not very good at being the recipients of kindness. Some may find it awkward to accept something for 'free', others embarrassed that they cannot return the favour. What lockdown has certainly brought to our attention is that it does not take much to make a difference. Neighbourhoods and communities have pulled together in ways unthinkable just a few short months ago. Freely giving up time to shop for others who are shielding, picking up the phone just to call someone who is living on their own, and clapping others with genuine sincerity from a million doorsteps. I do not think it is exaggerating to say this has been a social revolution.

The link between giving and the receiving of kind acts and our state of mental health is being practiced up and down the country today. My own college is really going for it. Not only are we having a special bulletin at the end of the week to showcase and celebrate the great work teachers and support staff have undertaken to support students; but senior managers have been asked to email five colleagues who have been kind to them, and thank them for it. The danger of this could be to compare emails received with your peers! I was delighted then to receive an email from a manager at our sister college in Croydon, thanking me for listening and accepting her ideas as we moved to a combined merged college group. This made my day. Simple as. What a lovely thing to say, and as it was out of the blue, it had genuine surprise appeal. Ok, that's *one*...come on comrades, where's the rest of the emails? It's my role to keep people happy and positive in the workplace, so no further emails means I'm not doing a great job! That is not the point Paul, move on.

It is not easy being kind in our rat race of a Western world, when work and home blurs into one stress ball and *time,* we tell ourselves, is always against us. Lockdown has changed this, the slowdown in pace resulting in more time to reflect. The big challenge to us all is what happens to that positivity once we emerge from this forced state of inertia? As the shackles are removed, the increased traffic and reintroduced leisure activities this week evidence this, will we just slip back into our time-poor methods of working? In one sense our mental health needs that routine and structure. Concern for our children's wellbeing against the risk of the number R increasing has been a fierce debate. As one of my favourite 1980s pop groups recorded, let's try to '*get the balance right*'. We can be busy and productive, but also find the time to be kind to ourselves and to others as part of our weekly routines.

The real challenge? Being kind to those who we are not usually bothered about. Those that look different, act different, sound different. *People who come from the wrong side of the tracks*. I for one need to work on this big time. If in doubt about the importance in doing this, check this out.

Be kind to one another, tender hearted, forgiving one another, as God in Christ forgave you. (Ephesians 4:32)

But love your enemies, and do good, and lend, expecting nothing in return, and your reward will be great, and you will be sons of the Most High, for he is kind to the ungrateful and the evil. (Luke 6:35)

But the fruit of the Spirit is love, joy, peace, patience, kindness, goodness, faithfulness, (Galatians 5:22)

And one verse not so familiar perhaps....
She opens her mouth with wisdom, and the teaching of kindness is on her tongue. (Proverbs 31:25)

Love that last one. *Kindness* – let's do it.

20th May: *Zoom – Unknown Territory*

Do you remember that great 1980s classic from Fat Larry's Band? Well little did they know how prophetic some of their lyrics would be in 2020: *'Then my whole wide world went zoom'*. Today I experienced three very different Zoom meetings, and as I sit here watching The Great British Sewing Bee, I feel very zoomed out.

The chosen digital platform of choice for the college is Microsoft Teams which has been the saviour for teachers and students alike in the past eight weeks. There have been more successes than failures with our quickly implemented remote learning strategy, and some students have actually excelled while studying from home where there is less peer distraction. Conversely, some students have really struggled since the lockdown because their home environment is not conducive to learning. As the Head of Teaching and Learning my role is to pull together 'what works' and 'what does not work' and share across the college learning community. I have had several meetings with different curriculum teams in past weeks to help me make informed judgements. What we do know is that apart from supporting the most vulnerable students based on Government guidelines, the Further Education sector is not expecting to open for business again this academic year. I am at this moment very glad to not do what the teaching staff up and down the country are required to do right now. That is, to grade each pupil or student based largely on what has been achieved before lockdown started. *Unknown territory.*

So back to Zoom. This was the meeting platform for an on-line meet up with the 'me's' around the country: those who are supporting the delivery in the new world of remote learning. The organiser, a respected education consultant in the sector, has termed this as the period of *pandemic pedagogy*. The participants were asked to reflect on ways in which their college has engaged with students using their Virtual Learning Environments of choice, and how they have kept teenagers interested in learning as the motivation begins to wane. The answer? Trial and error teaching...and lots of time chasing errant students. If that fails, contact the parents. If that fails focus on those who are still on the radar. As the consultant noted, this is probably the most radical change in the education landscape in our lifetime. *Unknown territory.*

My second Zoom meeting was with my side of the family. Dad is now a Zoom pro and Mum was on her best behaviour letting the rest of us chat away with usual sibling banter. The running joke being that my sister is going in every day as a key worker at The Children's Trust, while my brother and myself are in education working from home, and claiming we are just as busy - *happy to clap every Thursday on the doorstep.* 'Keep clapping' sis says, 'For just doing my job! I don't need claps; I need protective equipment today and a pay rise tomorrow!' *Our hero sister*; we all clapped her on screen enthusiastically.

'I've been busy all day reading emails in the safety of my own home' quips brother Rob. 'We can't risk going back to work. All those children carrying Covid' 'But happy to clap you sis!' You get the gist. Mum and Dad blended into the background being very used to the sibling banter, though the context was rather unusual, and maybe Lynne was actually offended by the throwaway quips? *Unknown territory.*

My final flutter with Zoom came straight after. Our church home group got together for its fortnightly catch up. Most of the group are senior citizens from the local community, so Diana and I feel quite young. So let's just say this spiritual foray into digital fellowship has been quite entertaining. With the Zoom time restriction of forty minutes always working against us, the conversation does not always flow smoothly. Wrong buttons are pushed, points have to be repeated several times, and varying levels of inter-connectivity quality end up making the whole event a mish mash of ideas, biblical interpretation and half-finished prayers when the time suddenly elapses. *Lost in translation* springs to mind. Yet despite these glitches something is going on with churches and Zoom that is quite a revelation. There were so many services using the Zoom App this Sunday, the system crashed in the USA and the UK. More people are tuning into on-line worship than go 'live' to a church building each week. The message of faith and salvation is reaching across the boundaries of the physical and meeting people right where they are. *Unknown territory.*

> *Bang, just one touch and all the church bells rang*
> *Heaven called and all the angels sang*

Breaking news: *'Can you hear me?'* becomes the most used sentence in the UK, followed by *'You're on mute'* and *'Is your camera on?'* *Unknown territory.*

21st May: *Taking the Shackles off*

Since Boris' disastrous address to the Nation on 10th May, which confused even the sharpest minds, folk have been edging back towards the outside world. The weather has been good, today reaching 28 degrees in the beautiful south, and the attraction of beaches and rural hotspots has been too much of a temptation for many. This is when the reliance on 'common sense' comes into play. Boris says, 'Be Alert' and for 99% of the population this is at the front of their thinking as they head for the coast and the great parks. The problem is that the tens of thousands of people about to descend on our tourist hotspots with good intentions, are arriving in their hoards *at the same time.*

The outcome was inevitable. The beaches in Devon were heaving this week. Traffic clogging up the narrow lanes - parking wardens having a field day. Beaches everywhere were flowing with visitors jockeying for position on the sands. Even my childhood home of Southend On Sea hit the headlines with pictures of large groups moving down the promenade, a tide of legs splashing against the shoreline. In the cities, the return to work for tens of thousands meant personal masks were firmly elasticated behind ears. Construction workers and those supporting the manufacturing industries were back on site or keeping two metres apart in factories. I got the impression the Government had relaxed the terms of the lockdown in the knowledge the tide could no longer be stopped. Frustration had boiled over into a hothead dash for freedom. The question on the screens and in the papers? Was this too fast, too soon, and what impact would this have on the magic R number?

Not since Brexit (remember that little nugget?) has an issue polarised opinion as much. Front line workers threw hands in the air with despair. The sick and vulnerable, especially those living and working in the care sector, were not impressed. Middle aged 'do-gooders' protested at the sheer stupidity of the 'younger generation', who were no doubt holding raves on street corners and warming their hands on roaring beach BBQs.

In the other corner, the 'let's get on with life' brigade shouted loudly about the need to protect jobs, bring in income, regenerate family life and enhance mental and physical health. The needs of the many perhaps are now greater than the lives of the few. Infection rates are down, hospital admissions falling fast, and death rates are declining. In London, there has not been one new recorded Covid case in the last 48 hours. The same story is happening across mainland Europe, while across The Big Pond, Donald Trump was exercising his presidential right to say and do whatever he wants. He is now taking an anti-malaria drug to fight off the virus when the evidence of any connection is unfounded and may even be dangerous to the taker. I won't print what my Diana said to that. Despite nearly 300,000 infections and 93,000 deaths, all of the 50 mainland States were easing their lockdowns. The unstoppable tide clearly winning the battle in the Land of the Free.

The picture outside of Europe and North America was a world of contradiction. In Australia and New Zealand, the impact of coronavirus has been negligible, and life has returned to near normal. Yet in South America hospitals in Brazil are close to collapse. Infection rates in Mumbai, India have soared. Stories are coming in of higher infection and death rates in poverty stricken areas in the Middle East and Southern Africa. We have not really touched on the impact of Covid-19 in the large refugee camps of Bangladesh, Kenya and South Sudan. Today, the World Health Organisation reported the largest increase in daily infection rates - 106,000. The overall number of cases now tops 5 million, with the death count at 326,000. While the Western democracies break free of their lockdowns, whether ready or not, most of the developing world has not even begun to see the peak of the pandemic.

The debate in the UK from this global perspective appears mundane in contrast. The shackles may be coming off in the richest nations, but the shackles of hell are only just tightening across the rest of planet Earth. To try and comprehend and rationalise why this is happening can be futile. All we can do is trust and pray for mercy, and hope that our own personal shackles of pride and fear do not win the day.

'Trust in the LORD with all your heart and lean not on your own understanding; in all your ways acknowledge Him, and He will make your paths straight." Proverbs 3:5-6

22nd May: *Class of '36*

'OK, cameras on, settle down quickly. We are continuing with Unit 4: *The History of Tourism*. Today's topic is The Airline Industry. Please take notes if that helps, but the full slideshow will be posted onto your Immersive Learning Cloud later. Trish, can you put your Box Vox away please. Josh, eyes front to screen, (types) *you are still on mute*.....thank you. Chelsea, you know the rules about cyber-texting in lessons - Google Glasses on silent please. Trish, we are still waiting. Thank you. Right, we can make a start.'

'Up until the Pandemic of 2020 air travel was very popular, and millions of people from the UK went abroad at least once a year. The most visited tourist destinations in Europe were what? ...Anyone?'

Is this before or after Brexit, Sir?'

'Good question Sharmila. The UK had left the European Union by then, though negotiations on trade deals were not all agreed. So, the main Summer destinations in Europe were?

'Spain, Sir. My mum said she went to the same resort for over 15 years. Think it was called Malinga, Sir'

'I think you mean, *Malaga* Josh. That was nice for your mum. Anyone else?

'Sir, why would you go abroad when you can go to Virtual World? Me and my boyfriend went last week. We had a lovely stay in Thailand. Dylan treated me to an Express Tan too. He's such a drool.'

'Thank you Chelsea, but we didn't have Virtual World in the Teens and Twenties. We had to travel by plane to get to where we wanted to go. Let me tell you about airline Economy Class.'

'Economic what, Sir? Was that the cheap seats? Couldn't you afford the posh deck, Sir?'

'Not very often Sharmila. Economy Class was a bit of a squeeze, I must admit. But before we got onto the plane everyone had to check in at least *two hours* before the flight departed, join long queues through security and customs, and wait for boarding to be announced in the airport lounge. Often, at peak times flights were delayed'

'Sounds like a real bore fest Sir. What was the point of all that if plane travel was so dirtshock?'

'Yes, well thank you Trish. I suppose with all that hanging around - we were so grateful to finally board the plane and get up in the air. We didn't care the leg room was cramped and the food tasted like plastic.'

'I read the Covid disease almost killed off the airlines totally, Sir?

'They never really recovered Claire, travel companies had £7bn worth of holiday refunds to give back to customers. Tens of thousands of jobs were lost in the industry in the Twenties. Companies like Shearings, Europe's largest coach tour operator, collapsed. It was a desperate time for workers in leisure and hospitality. The Government had to borrow over £60bn to keep the economy afloat.'

'My dad says we are still paying high taxes now cos of that. He blames *Boris the Borrower*. Did you vote for Boris Sir? My dad lost his job as a hotel boss. He was *furlonged*, or something? Millions lost their jobs as a result of the lockdowns.

'Is that why we are called the *Children of the Lockdown*, Sir? Nothing much else to do but....'

'...Ermm, thank you Chelsea. We get the idea! Sorry to hear about your dad Josh. As I said it was a really difficult time for everyone. We all had to stick together. We did get through it of course. It could have been a lot, lot worse though'

'What do you mean, Sir?

'We didn't have Donald Trump as our political leader during 2020!'

24th May: *Jigsaws*

I have never been a great fan of jigsaw puzzles. Not sure why, as I am a visual person who loves to look at picture art, who prefers using graphical images to communicate information, and do not even get me started on my love of maps. My career regret is that I would have loved to have been a cartographer.

It may be that jigsaws are just based on trial and error, granted with some degree of strategy, but they are in my eyes a little too mind numbing and tedious. Perhaps that is why they are so adored as a pastime. You can get lost in a jigsaw, a relaxing almost meditation-like experience that shuts off the stresses of the day. Maybe it is the pleasure of creating a picture one small piece at a time. A thousand-piece jigsaw could mirror the ten thousand brush strokes of a painter, who sees his or her masterpiece emerging right before their eyes. Perhaps that is it, jigsaw enthusiasts are just frustrated painters?

As part of this morning's Sunday service on Zoom, one of my dear church friends, another Graham, gave us an insight into his current home and work life under lockdown. As a work-from-home employee of a global engineering company, Graham speaks to colleagues from North America, Asia and Europe on a regular basis. He hears first-hand the hardship endured by families and communities worldwide, and regularly offers a listening ear and a kind word. During lockdown Graham and family have got to know some of their elderly neighbours a bit better, and this has provided the opportunity to offer a helping hand and friendly smile to the small community in which they live.

Unlike me Graham loves jigsaws, and to him every piece is a vital component. Each having its own worth and value, contributing to the final big picture. For Graham, although he is not sure if any of his kind words and deeds have an impact in themselves, every contribution provides a piece to the overall picture. A picture that we may not ourselves see or comprehend in full, but in faith we believe God *does*. We might not have all the answers to all the questions. We might not be able to see the complete story unfolding around us. But God *does*. In times of suffering as Christians we may certainly not have all the answers to explain why things are as they are. Yet, as Christians we can be more than purveyors of kindness. As Graham pointed out so pertinently, we may not have a monopoly on kindness, but we do have the monopoly on *hope*.

Pastor Graham continued with the theme of Transformation, exploring the experiences of the early Christian church in the book of Acts. I say 'church' but in First Century Judea the followers of Jesus met as a fluid moving community rather than gathering together within the confines of brick walls. This was the reality of a people finding their feet as they learned to share their worldly goods, as well as share the Good News to the world. Initially led by the apostle Peter, this church without walls was the very essence of community. Graham described them as a Learning Community, a Sharing Community and a Living Community. In my head I added, a *Transforming Community,* for their love and care for each other transformed the hearts and minds of those who lived around them. 'And the Lord added to their number daily those who were being saved' (v47).

At present, like many other congregations in the West, we are a church adapting to life without common walls. As such, we are being reminded that *church* is not the building in which we meet. After the formal service finished, we are put into Zoom chat rooms for a *virtual coffee* and catch up. This is important. It reminds us we are part of a community of believers. We cannot meet in person, but we are each a piece of a jigsaw, interconnected in prayer and hope. At the very end of the morning, we join up as one picture on screen, a gallery of small squares with familiar smiley faces. We become a jigsaw of believers at the click of a button. We may not know the story of each puzzle piece, but God knows not only this, but he also knows the complete picture. He is the painter of life. We are His Learning, Sharing, Living, Transforming church, with or without walls. He is the Master painter, and we are His Masterpiece. Amen to that.

25th May: *Trial and No Error*

Bank Holiday Monday - scorching weather, but the hottest story of the moment concerns Boris Johnson's chief adviser Dominic Cummings. It has transpired over the last few days that the man who is behind much of the Government's Covid-19 strategy has seemingly flouted the very same lockdown rules he helped to shape. The main accusation being that Cummings took his Covid symptomatic wife and young child from London to Durham to stay on his parents' farm estate so they could self-isolate. This was at the time when the strict instruction from No10 was to *Stay at Home*, especially for anyone with possible virus symptoms. This afternoon there was an unprecedented live press conference in the garden of 10 Downing Street where Cummings was grilled on his actions by journalists from all the major media organisations. And what a grilling it was. After Cummings read out a long statement explaining why he did what he did, one by one the journalists walked up to a microphone and fired their questions at the adviser. He was soon looking uncomfortable under the intense scrutiny.

Now this theatre piece might make great television, and the accusations of 'one rule for one, one rule for another' may be well founded, but it did have a sense of trial by media in a way we have not seen before in the UK. This man courts unpopularity, most famously by Remain supporters who saw him as the architect of the Leave campaign in 2016. He has been an integral part of the Conservative voting strategy for nearly twenty years, and in that time has criticised the established elite, the media, civil servants and the unions. He has also upset many in the Tory party with his views on their conduct and lack of intellect. Even the rather mild mannered David Cameron allegedly called Dominic Cummings a 'career psychopath'.

It is not be surprising therefore that the wolves are now circling at his door, all hoping for a bite of their intended victim. I even got the sense that Cummings had been left to hang out and dry, like dirty washing in the late afternoon sun. You could imagine Boris saying: *'your mess Dominic, publicly I will defend you, but you need to take the flack for it.'*

Oh, and this will be in public, on live TV and we'll invite a pack of wolves to interrogate you for an hour.' To his credit Cummings stuck firmly to his guns, even though the general consensus was he had driven roughshod over the spirit, if not the letter of the 'law'. This had rightly upset many who had made sacrifices to stay at home in very difficult family circumstances during the first part of the lockdown. As one senior BBC correspondent put it, 'the man respected by Mr Johnson for judging the public mood has made himself famous for falling foul of that opinion.'

One of the big winners of lockdown has been Netflix, the subscription channel that has seen a surge in subscriber numbers as people around the world seek additional home entertainment. From January to March 2020 16 million new accounts were reported. We already had an account, the American TV series catalogue being a big hit with Dan and Sarah. A new soon to be aired mini-series is forthcoming - Trail by Media. Six stories of famous trials that were inadvertently influenced due to the media attention they created. Even before the invention of social media, the C20th public showcasing of trial by jury grabbed the attention of millions.

Can you imagine if Jesus walked the Earth in 2020 and His crucifixion trial had been conducted in the glare of full media attention? Live on all terrestrial, satellite, and subscription channels! Jesus, standing in the dock, facing his accusers, as they lined up one by one waiting for their turn to strike.

'Is it true, you claim to be the son of God? 'How can you justify healing the sick on the Sabbath? 'Some of your followers call you the King of the Jews, what do you say to this? 'Are you the Messiah?

His friends had deserted Him, the full force of the populace media was against Him. Many on the fringes of power and those He had criticised in authority hidden in the background, orchestrating the mood of the crowds. Yet Jesus stood there in the knowledge His time had come, and he willingly submitted himself to the baying mob. Not once did He deny the charges made against Him. Why? Because they were all true. Jesus was guilty of being the Son of God. Guilty of healing the sick on the Sabbath. Unknown to his accusers, he was also the sacrificial Lamb, taking our sin on His shoulders. Instead of breaking the spirit and the letter of the Law, He was *fulfilling* it. Jesus was on trial, but in this case, there was no error. No lack of judgment, no misreading the public mood. As a result of the crucifixion, Jesus was no longer being judged, but the Risen Christ became the supreme judge of humanity. The table has turned.

How would we fare under the spotlight if our actions were scrutinised before the Son of God? As believers, the challenge is to answer the accusation: *'You have been a true disciple of Jesus'*, with: *'Yes your Honour, guilty as charged.'* It was another challenging and sobering thought.

27th May: *Can't Live Without.....*

Diana and I were taking the car for a slightly longer spin the other day and we came across a long line of traffic, stretching in front of us as far as the eye could see. I started to count this snake of stationery vehicles as we moved alongside. We passed 20, then 30, then 40 cars, mostly occupied by young people or parents with smaller children. As we came to the other end of the queue, I had counted at least 80 vehicles. What on earth could be so enticing that people would queue for this long, and in this heat?

You have probably already guessed - it was the re-opening of a MacDonald's Drive Thru, and the attraction of one's first Big Mac or Fillet O' Fish for two months was obviously too much to bear for the younger generation. It was a gobsmacking, jaw-dropping thought that this was something many people could not live without - and were willing to queue for hours just to sink their teeth into a double cheeseburger. I have been partial to the occasional Big Mac and fries myself, and as a parent there were occasions when I thought a Happy Meal was the best product on the High Street. But seriously, has lockdown really caused the British rank and file to lose their sense of priorities?

So as we worked our way through the death throes of this lockdown, emerging out the other side like hungry children in a cake store, I began looking at all the online posts which asked us to list what we had missed the most. The things we could not live without. What withdrawal symptoms have eight weeks of lockdown conjured up - either real or perceived? The obvious ones are going on holiday, eating out, seeing friends and relatives, visiting places of interest, socialising down the pub, and generally partying with the rest of the world. A more specific and touching one, which showed up in most Have Your Say posts and surveys, was *hugs*. So simple and yet such a basic human need. If you Google 'Quotes about Hugs', you would spend the rest of the day reading the vast library of examples. For my slightly reserved generation social hugs were not always expected, but now it is becoming the norm. Young people always seem to be hugging each other, in a genuine show of warmth and affection. That has got to be a good thing. So, as we come out of lockdown, I am challenging all middle-aged men to think seriously about this. Prepare to hug and be hugged! Hug your family, hug your friends (male and female), hug your neighbours, and hug anyone who just needs a hug. If in doubt. Hug.

The other 'can't live without...' and I think unless you are very 'folically challenged', this applies to most people, has been *hair cutting establishments*. The fact barber shops and hair salons in Italy were inundated with customers when they were allowed to re-open on 19th May proves the point. At No 34 we have had a range of strategies to overcome out-of-control hair growth, and the issue of *trust* has been at the heart of most of them. Dan, the hairiest of the household, has missed his fortnightly trip to the groomers the most. In response, he has signed up to the *DIY* approach, using Amazon bought clippers. Valiant effort, but after a couple of near ear misses he has resorted to letting it all grow out and is now waiting for his Turkish barber to come to the rescue. To his credit, after scalping himself into submission, he turned to his little stepbrother for further practice. The result on Daniel? Imagine the cartoon character Tin Tin with crew-cut attitude.

Next, Diana tackled my Anglo-Saxon thinning mop with the Dog grooming set. Result? Imagine Tin Tin as a middle-aged man with *no* attitude. On the top of my *'can't live without list'* therefore is Michelle, my hairdresser; a woman who can work miracles with a comb, hair grips, a water spray bottle and a hairdryer.

Astonishingly in the midst of lockdown, Diana was so peeved with her grey rooted haystack she gave up and turned to me for assistance. Now revenge is not in my nature, and I can honestly say that I tried my hardest to cut her tangled colossus. I was concentrating so much my tongue stuck out for the first time in years. Sadly, it was a cut too far, and despite viewing online tutorials, the end result was not flattering. Imagine a crow's nest with *lots* of attitude.

Thankfully, lockdown is easing, and shops have been told to reopen under strict social distancing guidelines. There will inevitably be long queues outside hair parlours up and down the country, probably all longer than the one we saw at the MacDonald's Drive Thru. But I will be there in neighbouring Bletchworth queuing to see the genius called Michelle. I would camp out all night outside her salon if that is what it takes, because I can no longer get away with wearing these stupid ribbons!

28th May: *Test and Trace*

I have already explained that my special superpower is to smell out animal faeces either from a distance of 50 metres or from the depths of sleep in the middle of the night. However, my wife rivals me in the sixth sense department with a track record in finding things on Gumtree that is nothing short of *spooky*. Take today for instance, we travelled to nearby Caterham-on-the-Hill to pick up items that had come onto the popular online trading site just this morning. All week we had discussed the need for new outdoor balls for Jess, and a new fence arrangement for Diana's garden allotment (I have already admitted that we are a middle class suburban family, so we are who we are!). Lo and behold, Diana found a lady who was selling, yep - several sports balls and wire fencing. Not only that, but the fencing fitted the exact length we needed for the allotment area. Jess was delighted with her new set of round and oval objects, which she can now systematically mutilate. The two of us spent the afternoon erecting a square wiry structure to protect paws (dog and fox variety) from trampling through the emerging shoots of carrots, strawberries and runner beans.

This ability of Diana's to trace exactly what we needed has been of great benefit to the household in recent years. In timely fashion, she has found unwanted concert tickets at knockdown prices to see The Corrs, U2, Coldplay and Take That. She has rooted out coffee machines, made to measure furniture, lampstands, an entire three piece suite (matching, from three different addresses), designer garden tools, fitted curtains with the right colour scheme, and just as we were giving up hope last Summer, she sourced Jess the Cockerpoo. The really, really eerie part? - *everything was local*.

I am hoping that the Government's new Test and Trace system, launched today, is going to be as reliable as Diana in finding what it needs to, and in timely fashion. With the magical 'R' number keeping below 1, and with infection and death rates still on the decline, Test and Trace is the next step in the fight against Covid-19. Similar systems are running in New Zealand, Germany and South Korea to name a few, the crux of which is to stop a large second wave of contagion from occurring.

If you now develop symptoms you arrange to have a Test. If positive, then a Contact Tracer gets in touch to discuss who you may have been in contact with. These people are then contacted by the Tracer who gives them the difficult news - *'Hi, you have been up close and personal with someone who has tested Covid positive. You now have to self-isolate for 14 days. Thank you for your time, goodbye.'* After the Dominic Cummings incident, a story which is still a thorn in Boris Johnson's side, the fear is that the public will not abide by these instructions. Cynics may even point to the timing of introducing Test and Trace as a means to deflect attention away from Cumming's misadventures in Durham.

The UK battle with coronavirus does appear to be in the balance. The R number could suddenly move upwards again and lockdown easing measures reversed overnight. In the Government briefing today we were told we can now meet up in groups of six, but only in gardens and private outdoor spaces. Loved ones, separated for months can now be together, if two metres apart still. To keep the nation's spirit up, messages on pub openings and the return of Premier League football in mid-June were well received. The return of dental services in two weeks' time was met with a personal leap of joy. A back molar has been giving me grief for days and getting me down in the dumps.

My sense of perspective returned as we clapped on the doorstep for the country's carers. According to the lady who initiated this social event, this could be the final time we do this. Fly on the wall reporting from a London hospital this week reminded us of the daily courage and professionalism of our front-line staff. Scenes of emergency care on coronavirus wards was hard armchair viewing. The physical suffering of the patients was matched by the mental and emotional anguish of the doctors and nurses. The daily death toll from Covid-19 in the UK is still in the hundreds; so, their personal sacrifice is far from over. We may now stop the clapping ritual, but the prayers for these amazing people will go on.

29th May: *The Dark Web*

Sadly, I am reading today about the growth in the number of online child abuse cases around the world, with child protection agencies warning that criminals and paedophiles are using the coronavirus lockdown to target children. In the UK, 300,00 people are considered a threat to children, and the Internet Watch Foundation claims nearly nine million attempts were made in April to access abuse websites which had been previously blocked. One of the reasons may be that, with fewer staffed hotlines in operation during the pandemic, site deletions from anti-abuse tech companies have significantly dropped. Hence barriers to these images have been well and truly breached. Of course, with many children spending far more time online in lockdown, they naturally become more vulnerable. Therefore, this so called 'dark web' activity preys on child isolation coupled with the increased lack of parental supervision.

In many pandemic hit economies, the situation is made worse with adults lured into the online child sex abuse industry because work elsewhere has dried up. The hope is that as the lockdown in countries eases, the re-opening of schools will provide a more secure natural safety net to millions of children. Back in the UK The National Crime Agency has created the ThinkuKnow website which gives advice to parents and others working with children on how best to protect them online. It has received more than 250,000 hits since the pandemic began.

This is such a reminder how technology can be both an opportunity for positive communication, but can also be used for the darkest of reasons. My Daniel and his friends are spending so much time online in the absence of formal schooling that today one of his friend's mum contacted the Year 11 parent's WhatsApp group, concerned about the effects of high screen time. I am thankful that Diana and myself do not have younger children in these strange times, who may be less streetwise in their thinking. Yet there is still a worry that these older teenage boys can view material that is damaging to their mental health, and exposes their immature views on violence and sex. This is one aspect of the *new normal* which will go under the wire if we are not super vigilant.

Excessive screen time of course is a worry in itself. When my Daniel met up with a small group of friends in the park this week, they tried to stick closely to being in their social pairings, but it was his remark when he returned that was poignant. When asked how being 'live' with his peers again was, he replied; *'we sat on the grass Dad just staring at each other, not sure how to act and what to say. It's so different to talking during online gaming. We'd all lost our social skills'.* Now the obvious comeback here was to question whether he or any of his 16-year-old male friends had any social skills in the first place. Nevertheless, it is their perception that counted here. They had at first hand experienced the impact of too much screen time during the two-month full lockdown.

As we are eased out of lockdown over the next few weeks, the darker side of the World Wide Web will be something we need to shed as much light on as possible. We must do all we can to stop our young people from becoming entangled, drawn into online conversations with strangers and enticed by the instant gratification that gaming can bring to the young mind. Like most parents, I have found this easier said than done, but working together and sharing information will go some way to providing an umbrella of protection. As with all challenges that we face, prayer is our greatest weapon. Here is one such prayer from beliefnet.com that challenged me to pray more for the post millennials we know.

O God, we pray and beseech you
To guide and protect our young people
From the dangers that are ever present in the world today.
Be with them as they experience
Sickness and health, sorrow and joy,
Loneliness and friendship, success and failure.
Gracious God give them the courage and the strength

To make the right decisions as they journey through life.
Through the power of the Holy Spirit,
May they come to know and experience your loving care.
We make this prayer through Christ our Lord.
Amen

30th May: *Reinventing the Wheel*

This may not be the picture across the whole of the UK, but I suspect it is. Everyone has gone bike mad during lockdown. The clear evidence for this is the enormous increase in the sales of bikes since late March, both for leisure use and for those who are looking for a new way to commute to work. With the amount of motor traffic down by around 90% this has made cycling feel much safer. Cycle-to-work schemes, family cycle rides around the local area, and upgrades for more serious cyclists have all added to the surge in sales. The Government is also ploughing £250m into cycling and walking initiatives, such as pop-up bike lanes and safer junctions for cyclists.

There is also a caveat here, with cycling experts warning of a greater risk to novice cyclists as the lockdown is eased, and more cars take to the roads. It is true many new cyclists at the moment look a little fragile, as they navigate city streets in heavier traffic this week. Today, Diana and I took Sarah up to Stratford in London so she could see her boyfriend Owen. He is the young man whose knowledge of C20th history had taken us to top spot in our weekly online quiz. They had not seen each other since the lockdown, and as the rules on meeting outside of your own household were relaxed, I offered to drive north of the Thames so they could spend some time together.

Living in a modern flat on the outskirts of the Queen Elizabeth Olympic Park, on arrival Owen led us through the open planned communal areas, so beautifully designed for the 2012 Games. With little traffic, this was a bike heaven for the locals. Even though there was an obvious lack of people walking around this usually bustling part of the city, there were bikes everywhere. Do you remember the Boris bike scheme when he was London Mayor? Yep, there were hundreds of these short-hire bicycles, zig-zagging their way across pavements and down thoroughfares. Owen, looking ahead to when he has to return to his London office, is on the lookout for a bike so he can join the *chain* gang.

While Diana and I took ourselves off to leave Sarah and Owen to catch up, we saw several people on bikes who were clearly new to pedal power. There was a nun who was getting into the cycling habit; a lady in full shalwar kameez attire working hard to stay upright, a larger man who was in the wrong gear so his legs were moving like a hamster on a wheel; and a couple on a tandem who reminded me of the Doctor Dolittle creature, the pushmi-pullyu. This also reminded Diana that she had been searching Gumtree to find a mountain bike for my Daniel, so he could cycle off road with his friends. Anything to get him off the X Box and do some exercise! She put her sixth sense to the test and found three in the Redhill-Reigate area. Brilliant. On contacting the sellers straight away, all three bikes had been snapped up already. It was a sellers' market. The world had gone second-hand bike crazy. This was going to test Diana's superpower to the limit.

The journey back through the Blackwell Tunnel was a slower affair, and I was thankful that I did not have to commute in and out of London like many of our friends. On finally returning home to leafy suburbia, we were met by a very excited Big Dan. *'You know I've been looking for a road bike? Well, I've found one on Facebook Market in East Grinstead - I'm first in the queue. The guy is going to hang on to it if we can pick up now.'* Dan is only insured on the family Peugeot 107 which is too small to pack in an adult bike, so he was waiting for us to return in the Hyundai i20. Jess the Cockerpoo had been a nightmare for the boys all day in our rare absence, so Diana stayed at home to care for 'our baby's very delicate needs'.

I drove Dan to East Grinstead to collect the bike before it went to the next bidder. At 6 O'clock I slumped on the sofa, mission accomplished. Somehow, I knew I would be dreaming of spinning wheels tonight.

A church pastor was stopped by a policeman at night for not having a back light.

In his defence the pastor says, 'I don't need a back-light Officer, the Lord is with me'
The policeman frowned, 'So there's two of you riding on this bike as well? You're nicked!'

31st May: *Explanation Ready*

One of the features of this surreal pandemic in the UK is the daily Government briefings held at Downing Street. In this briefing, Cabinet ministers, government approved scientists and medical advisors are subject to robust questioning from the media, political opponents and members of the general public. A spotlight of intense scrutiny that sometimes, as with the persistent questions about Dominic Cummings, lead to the questioning method overshadowing the debate substance. In riposte, the respondents on the whole stick to a tightly rehearsed text like Shakespearean actors not wavering from their script on stage. All this preparation means the minsters and their advisors are seemingly *explanation ready*. Ready for anything that is thrown at them. Yet being on script does not necessarily give the impression that real belief lies behind the message.

In our online morning service, the sermon was taken by Emily, the assistant pastor, sitting relaxed on her lounge sofa with Bible open on the coffee table. We were continuing the series from the Book of Acts, Chapter 3 v1-26, when the apostle Peter healed a lame beggar at the temple in Jerusalem. Seeing Peter and John coming his way, the beggar assumed they would give him money. Yet, without any silver or gold to their name, the disciples gave the man something far more valuable. Taking the man's arm, Peter told him to rise and walk in the name of Jesus. Immediately, the man jumped to his feet with strength returning to his ankles. It was not long before a crowd gathered to watch in amazement and bewilderment. Peter knew what questions were on the tips of their tongues, and he preceded to explain with great assuredness where the source of this healing had come from. He explained with total conviction the events leading up to the crucifixion, and how the resurrection of Jesus tied into the prophecies foretold in the Jewish Torah.

By faith in the name of Jesus, this man whom you see and know was made strong. It is Jesus' name and the faith that comes through him that has completely healed him, as you can all see. (v16)

This was not just a passionate speech to explain how healing can happen in the name of Jesus, but the witness of a man who had walked and talked with the risen Christ. This was more than just an explanation of historical events. Here, Peter's declaration of faith is the testimony upon which God's Church on Earth has been built for the past 2000 years. Now that is being *explanation ready!*

To further emphasise our need to be ready to explain our faith to others, Emily used a famous sermon from one of the great Baptist Pastors of the C20th, S. M. Lockridge. Here are some of the words from what is regarded to be one of the great sermons of all time, *'That's my King! Do You Know Him?':*

I wonder if you know him? Well, my King is the King.
He's the key to knowledge
He's the wellspring to wisdom
He's the doorway to deliverance
He's the pathway to peace
He's the roadway to righteousness
He's the highway to holiness
He's the gateway of glory

These are words that are certainly clear and bold. They leave nothing to the imagination, yet they are everything that we should imagine our God to be. Emily has challenged us to be more than just 'good', greater than mere 'kindness', and more than just keeping to the script when explaining our faith to others. To be explanation ready for God's Kingdom, we need to have total courage in our convictions - not only by giving out the words from our mouth but sharing out the love of the risen Christ from our hearts. This is the *explanation ready* we have to aspire to.

Lottie: a cat with more than nine lives

Bluebell heaven: a lockdown walk in nearby woods

Spot the difference! Mo the Maine Coon being extra photogenic.

'This is harder than I remember!' Diana reliving past glories on a swing

Jess 'helping' me raise money for the 2.6 Challenge

Family lockdown Zoom call. 'Dad you're still on mute!'

Picnic in suburbia. A rare communal gathering to celebrate VE Day

Puppy love! Jess, our lockdown treasure.

Dan, Sarah and Daniel enjoying the long hot lockdown Summer.

Collateral damage!

Diana's greenhouse project. Didn't she do well?

The allotment. Or is it a caged rainforest?

Mo checking my efforts to work from home are up to scratch!

Mr and Mrs Pidgeon taunting Jess with their daily roof top dance

The Lighthouse. Jess knows how blessed we have been.

Twilight descends over the nature reserve.

Jess taking me for a walk along the water's edge.

JUNE 2020

1st June: *Manic Monday*

A significant Covid-19 day in many ways, and never has the Bangles song title of 1986 been so nationally poignant. In the UK, further lockdown easing measures are introduced, the key one being the opening of nursery and primary schools in England for nursery age, Year 1 and Year 6 age groups. Although the death rate from coronavirus continues to show a gradual decline, the number of new infections remains stubbornly high. Government figures note about 2,000 per day, though independent assessments insist this figure is much higher. Teachers' unions point to this discrepancy, while scientists have uttered their concerns; but today many schools were doing their best to accommodate these year groups. Parents have been forced to choose between the benefits of a return to formal education for their children, against the risk, however small, of infection. In the end, day one of re-opening saw a 50/50 split - with half the expected pupils turning up for school. Parents who opted to keep their children at home wait in the wings to see if this is a necessary risk to take or not. The front page picture on the London Evening Standard of a teacher wearing a mask and a visor taking the temperature of one pupil was both reassuring and horrific at the same time.

Another easing measure is more confusing than anything else. Each part of the UK has slightly different rules about how we should now meet others, though in each case the two metre social distancing rule still applies. In England, the new guideline on meeting others states you can now meet up with up to six others, anywhere outdoors. In Scotland, you can meet up with eight others but from just two different households, anywhere outdoors but ideally within five miles. In Wales it is any number of people but from two households, within a five mile distance on your locality; and in Northern Ireland you can meet up to six people, anywhere outdoors. Got it? Quite a few unsurprisingly did not.

Over the weekend in the glorious sunshine crowds gathered on beaches, in parks, and in the centre of London where a protest to support black communities in the USA was held. There was certainly no attempt at social distancing in Trafalgar Square. These scenes re-energised the debate on whether we were coming out of lockdown too quickly. In fact, several of the government advisory Sage committee members wanted the test and trace system fully operational with cases coming down significantly before these sorts of measures were introduced. First time 'off-script' for some!

And then there is the re-introduction of live sporting events. After 76 days, horse racing returned, starting with a meeting at Gosforth Park, Newcastle. Races were limited to 12 runners, masks were worn by the jockeys, and a range of one-way routes around the paddocks and the parade ring were observed. Winners were not greeted by the noise of a watching crowd, rather the muted applause of owners and trainers. At Milton Keynes, snooker returned behind closed doors shown on free-to-air TV. The Championship League resumed, with players isolating themselves for 18 hours after being given a Covid-19 test. Keeping two meters apart at all times, players were also barred from sharing the same equipment. Cricket, Formula 1, rugby, and Premier League football are all due to return in the coming weeks.

With so many people ardently trying to discover what the *new normal* means in practice, this could be the end of our enforced period of reflective melancholy. The slow-down will soon become the rat race again, and for all the challenge and hurt that coronavirus has brought, we will perhaps look back at the Spring of 2020 with some envy in the future. Perhaps *Manic Monday* was not the only 1980s pop reference here. Perhaps *Blue Monday* by *New Order* is far more apt.

2nd June: *It Must Be Love!*

The Gumtree guru strikes again! Step-mum finds bike for grateful 16-year-old.

Redhill resident and Gumtree expert, Diana Banthorpe has done it again! Under immense pressure to find the right bike at the right price, in a second-hand market that has gone ballistic, Diana swooped into action this week with the speed and precision of a Harley Davidson. *'It has been the biggest challenge of my Gumtree career'*, she said, *'bikes are going like hot cakes out there, and I was beginning to doubt my special sixth sense on this one!'* However, Diana did not have to wait for long before locating a 26 inch wheel Rockhopper mountain bike for her teenage stepson. *'We had to move fast - by the time we picked it up the lady had already had 15 other enquiries'* she told The Gazette.

Despite the success, Diana was left disappointed. *'I set myself very high standards, and it was a shame we had to do a 20 mile round trip to Crawley this time. Usually I find items we need in the next street.'* The happy teen Daniel was unable to comment today due to 'extensive sleeping arrangements', but a spokesperson close to the family told The Redhill & Reigate Gazette, *'Woof, woof, woof...growl...woof woof woof.'*

The week's Gumtree drama did not stop there. I was hard at work in my makeshift bedroom-office in yet another Microsoft Teams meeting when Diana burst in with all the excitement of a kitten finding a ball of wool smelling of catnip. It was a good job I was on mute and off camera. Apparently, my wife, who is slowly losing a number of plotlines, has been looking for a fruit cage to protect her beloved allotment from hungry pigeons. It needed to be two metres square with a height to accommodate her own five-foot stature once standing inside. *Of course*, Diana had found one on Gumtree and seller-buyer contact had already been made. Once I had finished this online meeting it would be off to nearby Dorking to collect.

On arrival at the rural cottage location we were greeted by a middle-aged couple and three gorgeous Labradors. *'Aaahhh, you have one of each!'*, Diana cried. The chocolate one reminded us of our late family dog Keedra, soft fur and gentle nature. The black lab strutted around their garden like an Emperor surveying his kingdom; and then there was the tan coloured one. Koda was a rescue dog this couple had brought back from Cyprus. In the six months since, Koda had kept himself to himself. But then as we entered the back garden, he fixed his eyes on me. The next twenty minutes were a challenge for Diana and the two sellers as they tried to dismantle the huge fruit cage whilst keeping to social distancing. For me, there was not an ounce of social distancing going on.

While chocolate and black frolicked on the lawn, my new friend Koda was all over me like the proverbial rash. This large lab was actually trying to cuddle me, enveloping my small frame in his front claws. Once I had wrestled him to the floor, he just wanted the ultimate tummy tickle. Every time I tried to move, Koda grabbed me again, gooey eyes staring up at me like I was the 'one and only'. The others just laughed, Koda's owners in sheer disbelief. They suggested that perhaps I resembled someone in Cyprus who had meant a lot to Koda.

I just wanted them to dismantle the cage, complete the deal and make a quick escape. As attractive as Koda thought I was, the old trick of *'here boy come, biscuits...biscuits...'* gave me the break I needed. Hyundai loaded with poles and netting, I sped out of there like....a man escaping from a crazy love sick hound. Diana did not help matters by singing 'Puppy Love' and 'Hound Dog' on the way home.

At least she was happy with her fruit cage. I smelt like canine body odour and then noticed I had visible claw marks running down both legs from knee to ankle. I am not sure what happened back at the Labrador love factory, but I was pleased to get home and give Jess a big cuddle, feeling guilty I had just had a dangerous liaison with another dog. Next time we do a collection, I will check with Diana if any love sick pets are resident waiting to pounce.

4th June: *The Perfect Storm (Part 1)*

The idiom, 'the perfect storm' was initially taken from the non-fiction book of the same name written by Sebastian Junger in 1997. Junger recounts the story of the Andrea Gail, a commercial fishing boat lost at sea with all its crew, due to a unique confluence of storms off the Massachusetts coastline. The story is more famously known as a hit movie released in 2000 starring George Clooney. In modern speech, the term now refers to any situation where a rare combination of circumstances come together at the same time to create a catastrophic event.

This exact scenario seems to be playing out in the USA at present, a country which has seen an escalation of events in the past week that has in turn led to a worldwide backlash against cultural and institutional racism. On 25th May a black man George Floyd died whilst being arrested by four white policemen in Minnesota. The nine minutes in which one of the officers knelt on his neck restricting Floyd's airways was captured on camera. Floyd's last words, 'I can't breathe', have become synonymous with what has followed. Protest marches have erupted across the States, thousands of people from all ethnic groups joined by fellow white Americans, sending a clear message to the Whitehouse, that *Black Lives Matter*.

Sadly, many of the marches have descended into running street battles between protestors and state police, supported by the National Guard. Peaceful demonstrations provoked into becoming more violent ones. For many black Americans George Floyd's death is the last nail in the coffin, many giving emotional testimonies into how tired and anguished they feel at the obvious inequalities that exist. The statistics back up their claims. Black Americans are more likely to be shot and killed by the police; are more likely to get arrested for drug crimes; and more likely to end up in state prisons. The result? The largest protest against racial oppression since the 1960s.

This outcry of injustice comes at a time when the coronavirus pandemic continues to sweep across the USA killing many. As in the UK, a disproportionate number from black and ethnic communities are dying. Millions are now claiming unemployment welfare as a direct result of the lockdown; many from economic-poor black and ethnic communities. So, tens of thousands march, some with headscarves and crudely made protective facemasks, many without. Masses of people gathering in confined urban spaces. The fear of contagion now surpassed by the anger and even hatred felt against state authorities and the federal government.

These scenes have now been repeated in the UK, Germany, France and Australia. An initial response to the death of one man, but an ever-growing collective response to the treatment of people of colour around the World. This 'right to protest' in large numbers appears to contravene the rules on social distancing here too. Last Saturday 3,000 people demonstrated in the heart of London - a sea of banners moving through narrow roads ending up in Trafalgar Square; the police, with little grounds or means to 'move them on'. Time will tell if this action has a detrimental impact on infection rates.

To complete the perfect storm in the United States we have the President. Today, ex-US Defence secretary James Mattis denounced Donald Trump's handling of the protests as being deliberately divisive. There is no doubt Trump has added fuel to the fire; firstly by calling the protestors criminals and thugs, and then by his actions three days ago outside the Whitehouse. After peaceful protestors were dispersed with tear gas and rubber bullets from a park close by, the President crossed the park to an historic church for a photo opportunity. Bible sitting unnaturally in his right hand, Trump stood there as if he was being ordained with renewed moral purpose. It was meant to be a symbol of leadership in a God fearing country. Critics from both religious and secular leanings saw it as staged and vulgar. As a result, the protests have become bigger and louder.

Whatever feelings one may have towards President Trump, looking from the outside in, the most powerful country on Earth is now badly wounded. The perfect storm has hit, and the reaction of many is to kneel and pray. Let us all pray that this storm will pass, and the American people will find healing and justice in the months ahead - maybe for the first time in decades.

5th June: *The Perfect Storm (Part 2)*

Yesterday I used the idiom 'The Perfect Storm' in its metaphoric sense. Today I am referring to it in its literal sense. I have read in the news lately about a series of tropical cyclones around India, mostly building up and then carrying out their full force of destruction in the Arabian Sea and the Bay of Bengal. The worst of these was a super cyclonic storm that tore through eastern India and Bangladesh in May. The city of Kolkata in West Bengal experienced 115mph winds, buildings collapsing, and electricity power completely cut. Nearly three million people had already been evacuated from there and in neighbouring Bangladesh. It was the most severe storm to have hit the region in 20 years, and although there were relatively few fatalities, the financial cost to the region's infrastructure (we know now) would be the highest ever. All this on top of Covid-19, with the need for effective social distancing hampering the already over-stretched authorities.

This week a similar strength cyclonic storm headed for Mumbai on India's western coastline. A city of huge population density stood in the path of the storm, the first to threaten the country's economic capital since 1948. Again, a region already overwhelmed by the Covid pandemic was preparing for the worst. As it hit landfall, the storm suddenly veered to the east and by passed the city, leaving most of the population unscathed. Heavy lashings of rain and high winds brought inconvenience rather than the expected travesty. In a short space of time it was the tale of two cities in India fighting for survival, and a tale of national destruction in Bangladesh.

In the UK we are blessed to have a more moderate temperate climate. However, the C21st has brought a mix of flooding and irregular heatwave patterns, with records being seemingly broken on a frequent basis. Before lockdown we endured the wettest February on record, and we have just experienced the sunniest month - by a country mile! However, my thoughts turn to the Great Storm of 1987. I was studying at the Roehampton Institute near Wimbledon at the time, living in student on-site accommodation. I can remember two things. The site of uprooted trees flying across Wimbledon Common like wooden missiles and waking up the next morning to find a large oak tree lying outside my ground floor room window. The outside wall damaged, another metre and it would have crashed through the window and onto my bed. Since then, strong windy conditions have always frayed my nerves. After seeing first-hand how destructive nature can be, I remain fearful of high winds to this day.

Faith, not fear. That is the message of the New Testament. The phrases 'fear not' and 'be not afraid' appear nearly 100 times in the Bible. Perhaps the most famous passage to echo this sentiment is found in Matthew, Mark and Luke, when Jesus calms the storm on the Sea of Galilee. Jesus has just given a series of sermons, preaching to a large crowd from a boat pushed a short distance into the water. He then tells the disciples to take them all to the other side of the lake because He knew another calling awaited in the form of a demon-possessed man. Halfway across, a storm suddenly arose, and soon swirling winds and crashing waves engulfed the boat. Despite being experienced fishermen, the disciples feared for their lives and turned to Jesus, who was sleeping soundly in the stern. The fact Jesus was sleeping is full of significance, in itself. For Jesus was fully human, exhausted after hours of public speaking; yet He is also fully divine, secure in the knowledge He is at one with the Creator. He is fully faithful in the power bestowed on Him by the Father.

On waking Jesus, the disciples plead, 'Teacher, do you not care that we are perishing?'
These are the men who have been with this man at close quarters. They have witnessed His divinity many times, yet they, in their full humanity are consumed with fear. At once, Jesus gets up and rebukes the wind and the raging waters. The storm subsides, and all is calm. He turns then to His disciples and asks the simplest yet most pertinent of all questions. 'Where is your faith?'

Whether we find ourselves in a metaphoric storm like the American people, or in a literal storm like the people of India and Bangladesh, we have to ask our self the same question. Do we place our faith in politicians, scientists and climatologists? Do we place our faith in the technology that surrounds us? Do we fall back to our default fear button like the disciples in the boat? Or do we place our faith in the Creator of all things; the God of mercy and grace? If we cling onto fear, then we cannot expect to feel the hope promised to every one of us. Surely placing our faith in the One who can calm every perfect storm will open our eyes to the possibilities and plans that God has for us all.

6th June: *Behind the Mask*

The UK Government has changed its mind. The wearing of masks is now an officially endorsed method to stop the spread of Covid-19, and the English public must now wear one on public transport and in indoor spaces where social distancing is not possible. This comes into force on the 15th June to allow time for everyone to either make their own or purchase one from a reputable source. Along with the new forthcoming quarantine rules for those entering the country, the question on the lips of commentators and critics is, *why were these measures not introduced earlier?* The magic R number in some parts of the North East and the South West is reported to be moving above the critical '1', and infection rates elsewhere are still higher than hoped for. It is argued, if borders had been tightened in March, if masks had been made compulsory in at least April, surely the garden would be rosier than it is now?

Lockdown easing has led to high numbers visiting coastal towns and rural hotspots. Now with the escalation of anti-racist protest marches in our major towns and cities, twelve days on from the killing of George Floyd in Minnesota, the 'crowd' problem has dominated the headlines. Today several thousand marched on the US Embassy near Vauxhall, London. Many wore masks but again, many hundreds did not. Cabinet and Opposition Ministers were balanced in their comment about, 'the right to raise voices' but not at the expense of the safety of self and others. Unfortunately, clashes between police and some protestors occurred near Downing Street, with missiles and fireworks thrown at officers. The Metropolitan Commissioner Dame Cressida Dick was 'appalled' by the scenes which resulted in 14 police injuries and 14 arrests. The counter-protestations are also escalating.

Yet there is growing defiance from protest leaders who talk about the world pandemic of racism as a more significant force than coronavirus. The Bishop of Dover, Rev Rose Hudson-Wilkin, the Church of England's first female black bishop, goes as far as claiming racism is killing people...' and sadly the world pays no attention'. The message to those in authority is profound - *we might as well stand up and be heard, for the risk in not doing so is greater.* The death of George Floyd has lifted the mask off the face of the world. It is ironic as we start to cover up our individual faces as a part of everyday life, we also need to make sure the mask of prejudice and judgement has been well and truly removed. There can be no more excuses. No more wearing of public facing masks that hide any thoughts of discrimination. This is a huge challenge to all societies from every corner of Earth, for now, and as and when we emerge from the ashes of Covid-19.

7th June: *40*

This has been a year when numbers have been part of everyday life. It started in January with the birth of a new decade. 2020 is a special year as it is the only year you are likely to live through wherein the first two digits will match the second two digits. So if you make 101 as of now, you will see in the year 2121. Good luck. Since then we have been bombarded with statistics of new Covid-19 cases around the world, weekly death tolls, and complex comparisons between national figures. The British public have had to endure more line graphs and pie charts at Government daily briefings than is good for the soul. Who said the maths you learn at school will never come in useful?

So the numbers this week that have grabbed the attention remain a sombre reminder that millions of people are mourning loved ones around the world.

There are now over 400,000 recorded coronavirus related deaths.

In the UK, the recorded death toll has now exceeded 40,000.

At least 4,000 people have died from Covid-19 in care homes in England.

A survey in May suggested 1 in 400 people in England could have Covid-19 at any given time.

And I am going to continue with a song written by one of my favourite bands. Inspired by the Psalm of the same number, U2 recorded this as the last track on their album War in 1983. The song brings back memories of a then teenager wrestling with his faith. It also echoes the heartfelt cry of many who feel lost, and hope for a brighter song in future.
This is 40.

I waited patiently for the Lord
He inclined and heard my cry
He brought me up out of the pit
Out of the mire and clay
I will sing, sing a new song
I will sing, sing a new song
How long to sing this song
How long to sing this song
He set my feet upon a rock
And made my footsteps firm
Many will see
Many will see and fear
I will sing, sing a new song
I will sing, sing a new song

8th June: *Quarantine*

Thank you, sir, could you please move forward to the yellow line. And, yes your family can move there too. Thank you. That's great. Now if I can see all your passports.

Here you go.

Thank you. I see you have travelled from Australia. Who did you fly with may I ask?

KangaAir

I hear the flights can be a bit...jumpy.

I'm sorry?

Apologies Sir, just my British sense of humour. Are you here for business or pleasure?

Quarantine.

Oh right Sir, of course. It's just a habit to ask that question. And how long will you be staying in quarantine for?

For the full two weeks. Unless the rules have changed since we took off 23 hours ago?

Afraid not Sir. Two weeks it is. You will be in quarantine for the whole of that time. Have you filled in the form to verify your intended accommodation address?

Yes, here. We will be in private accommodation in Kew. It's my brother's flat. He's flown the other way to see our parents in Sydney. I think he's got the best deal here! Amy, Brad, quiet please, nearly finished.

Well Sir, there's so much to do in London, for all the family, even lively teenagers. If you were not in quarantine that is. You could always look up the attractions online, and pretend to visit them? I recommend the 360 degree virtual tour of the Victoria and Albert Museum.

My brother informed me as we landed that his internet has been cut off. Roadworks!

Well Sir, being in Kew, I'm sure he has a nice garden?

Nope. Just a small patio. It's going to be the trip of nightmares.

Well, look on the bright side Sir, you could be quarantined in Croydon! Let me just remind you that if you break quarantine, you could be fined. You can leave the flat for essential items...like food, and fresh air. Your passports are fine. May I warmly welcome you to the United Kingdom. Enjoy your visit.

Next please.....

10th June: *Rhythm and Blues*

The hot dry spell has left us. The rain is teaming down my office-bedroom window as I try to work out how teaching staff at the college can best use the three weeks up until the summer break. Although some Primary schools are *edutaining* random selections of pupils, most of the education sector is still closed. Next week, a few students will attend the college to carry out practical assessments or written tests where evidence of knowledge and skills is still required. A skeleton staff team will preside over this, but my presence is not a requirement.

Diana, who works at the neighbouring sixth form college, is unlikely to return to her office before September either. Her teaching support role has been essentially quashed by lockdown and she is feeling somewhat lost and redundant. However, knowing how I am still stuck in a daily Deja vu loop with my laptop screen, she keeps herself busy; planting, sewing, tiling, walking the dog, cleaning, cooking cakes, grooming the dog, searching for items on Gumtree, painting outside walls....and buying ever more expensive treats...for the dog. This is all fine, but despite some small social distancing gatherings in gardens, overall we are all beginning to go a bit stir crazy. The onset of gloomy skies is not going to help matters as we approach 12 weeks in lockdown.

In the past week, Diana went all the way to Crawley to buy the nine terracotta tiles needed to complete the refurbishment of the side passage. She paid a fiver and came back with a box of rubble that Trades Description would have a field day with. The other day she left the hose on in the back garden and although the resulting paddling pool was welcome in the heat, the grass took a battering. Sarah, soon to be moving to her new student house in Reading, is obviously missing Owen and her mind is often away with the proverbial fairies. For lunch last Saturday, she cooked us all fishfinger rolls. A firm favourite. Unless the fishfingers appear on the plate less cooked than the roll that holds them. I am not a fan of sushi in breadcrumbs. As ever, it was the thought that counted.

It is difficult to tell if teen Daniel is losing the plot, as he continues to abide by the same on screen, late to bed, late up, on screen, eat, on screen routine. He has been out on his new mountain bike and has enquired whether everyone else is ok.... twice! That's progress. Big Dan is still recording his radio shows in the corner of his bedroom; but despite a new online love interest and regular garden work outs, is becoming more and more twitchy. This week he has swapped the exercise mat for the sofa, to watch every episode of Life on Mars and Ashes to Ashes. Great retro viewing, but essentially a story of two people living in a parallel universe whilst in comas. Too close to current reality for my liking.

I have reached *routine numb equals acting dumb* stage. Yesterday I put a box of cereal in the fridge and the milk in the cupboard. I am also looking more like a tired unshaven rock artist whose hair is trying to revive past days of glory. Which is why the solution to our shortcomings presented itself like a fluorescent blimp floating above house No 7, with a gigantic neon sign pointing to the garage below. Dan and I had discussed buying a drum kit at the start of lockdown, but with room space tight and other priorities (like the greenhouse!) we let it go. Until now! The lady at No 7 was storing her old Stagg kit in the garage ready to be sold. Rusty, full of cobwebs and sounding like it looked, £20 was agreed and after a little TLC it now takes pride of place...in Sarah's bedroom. Sarah is now considering moving out earlier.

I used to play in my twenties, Dan bashes a drum kit like there's no tomorrow, and I am hoping my son will also use this opportunity to learn a new skill. Instead of shooting zombies he too can unleash his inner angst on the skins and the one battered cymbal. So a win-win situation I think. The three males can channel some energy, Sarah can thank us for making her mind up about moving out, and Diana can do her tasks, relaxing to the steady thump of happy rhythms. One thing we did not take into account though. Jess, whose canine hearing far exceeds our own, can hear when one of us is on the kit from several miles away: and subsequently starts howling like a werewolf with its foot caught in a mantrap. The harmony hoped for would require greater thought.

I am going to leave it a while before I buy a new louder crash cymbal.

11th June: *Statues*

Knock! knock!

Who's there?

Statue

Statue who?

Statue I saw standing on the plinth in town yesterday?

Aah, the old ones are the best. Or, perhaps 'old' is no longer the virtue it once was? As a result of the global anti-racist protests, hurt and anger has been channelled against historical figures of the past who once symbolised the atrocities of the international slave trade. In Bristol, a statue of 17th Century slave trader Edward Colston was torn down during a Black Lives Matter protest and thrown into the nearby river. Colston trafficked tens of thousands from Africa to the Americas, and although he ploughed his wealth back into the Bristol community, sustaining schools, alms-houses and churches, his legacy has remained divisive. A petition to remove it had garnered more than 11,000 signatures. It said:

"Whilst history shouldn't be forgotten, these people who benefited from the enslavement of individuals do not deserve the honour of a statue. This should be reserved for those who bring about positive change and who fight for peace, equality and social unity."

Other statues have now been targeted by demonstrators. Perhaps one of the most known is the statue of Cecil Rhodes at Oxford University. A 19th Century businessman and politician, he represented white supremacy in southern Africa. Today, a statue of Robert Baden-Powell, the founder of the Scouts movement, is to be removed from Poole Quay near Bournemouth amid fears it is on a target list for attack. Campaigners have long accused Baden-Powell of racism, homophobia and being an open supporter of Hitler. There has been an immediate reaction from those who have seen Baden-Powell as a positive role model, enabling millions of young people to have a real sense of purpose through joining the Scouts movement. Across the Atlantic, statues of politicians who were from a Confederacy background like President Jefferson Davis, and those associated with colonialism such as explorer Christopher Columbus have been torn down in Richmond and Boston respectively.

This course of action begs the question - how should we treat those whose values reflected the age they lived in rather than the core values of today? Should they be kept in the public eye to remind us of our past, irrespective of their chequered attributes, or do we remove them from view, hidden in a dusty museum or in a warehouse crate? If it is the latter, where do we then draw the line? Other artforms and pieces of literature have already come under scrutiny. The popular 90's TV show Little Britain has been taken off Netflix and BBC iPlayer due to its portrayal of people of colour. As I write there are calls to do the same with the cult sitcom Gavin and Stacey, in which gags relating to colour and sexual orientation were common. The biggest cull in the States has been the 1939 Oscar multi-award winning film "Gone With The Wind" for its romanticising of slavery.

During his race to the Whitehouse in March 2008, Barack Obama paraphrased the famous line from novelist William Faulkner's Requiem for a Nun; *'The past is never dead. It's not even the past'*. Obama was referring to the way in which history never really goes away as it has shaped the way we live today. In this sense the issue of racism and specifically the slave trade both in North America and in Europe may have an historical context, but it's legacy is all around us in the living and breathing present, and continues to permeate society in the here and now. What we need to decide as a collective of democratic nations is how we wish to tackle in built prejudice in the new normal. The legacy of Covid-19 will also one day be part of our historical past, but if Faulkner is right, then its impact will always be in our present.

13th June: *I'm Forever Blowing Bubbles*

In my eyes Sarah's boyfriend of four months Owen has a lot going for him. He seems a kind, intelligent and hard-working young man. His contribution to our online Friday quiz night has given us back to back victories. Needless to say, since Owen last played with the Flufighters, we have struggled to reach those dizzy heights again. Owen's family live near Grays in Essex, the county of my birth and my formative years. Added to this Owen has now more recently moved to a flat in Stratford, just a short walk from The New London Stadium. This is significant because it is the adopted home of West Ham United Football Club, my Premier League team. My parents originally came from the East End before moving out to Southend-on-Sea in the early 1970s, the Hammers are therefore firmly ingrained into our family history. Though you can now also guess where my footballing heart lies when it comes to following a club week in week out. Currently a somewhat tragic association. So, for me, Owen ticks a lot of boxes, and now today he is providing a sanctuary for my stepdaughter as a result of another lockdown easing directive from the Government. With the arrival of the drum kit, the timing is impeccable.

The new lockdown easing rule allows those living on their own to form a *support bubble* with another household. Or in reversal, someone from one household can now be with someone living on their own. This means those who have been in solitary lockdown can be with loved ones. So instead of waiting to move to her university house in July, Sarah can move in to keep Owen company up in East London. Bags packed and on the train before you could say 'I'm forever blowing bubbles', Sarah left the house with smiles and relief in abundance. Within five minutes of her departure her brother is on the drum kit thumping along to The Foo Fighters' *Learn To Fly*.

I have always wondered why West Ham fans sing the bubbles song. Apparently, the original song was written for a 1918 Broadway musical called 'The Passing Show'. This in itself seems apt given the legacy of West Ham's so called *academy of beautiful passing football*. Having been well established as a popular song in London music halls in the 1920s, a local headmaster and Hammers fan introduced it to the club and then subsequently the die-hard supporters. At the same time, one of his own school pupils played for the team adopting the nickname 'Bubbles'. Every time 'Bubbles' excelled on the pitch, Headmaster Cornelius Beal would break into the song. Somewhere along the line *'I'm Forever Blowing Bubbles*' stuck in the mindset of fans at the Boleyn Ground, and it gradually became synonymous with the First Team after the second world war.

> *I'm forever blowing bubbles,*
> *Pretty bubbles in the air,*
> *They fly so high,*
> *They reach the sky,*
> *And like my dreams they fade and die!*
> *Fortunes always hiding,*
> *I've looked everywhere,*
> *I'm forever blowing bubbles,*
> *Pretty bubbles in the air!*

As you can read, the sentiment of the lyrics is one of hope and a promise of a better future, only for these dreams to eventually be dashed. You would expect a terrace chant to offer a bit more encouragement! With just a handful of trophies in the cabinet since the song's introduction, there is a strong argument that 'Bubbles' has turned out to be somewhat of a curse rather than a blessing! Yet, for West Ham fans, like so many sports fans around the world, hope springs eternal. Blind optimism keeps the hope alive. It is a well-known adage in footballing circles, that it is not your team losing that hurts the most, *it is the hope of better to come that kills you.* Like so many other facets of our modern lives, sport is a fickle beast, and putting your faith and hope in something that has such a flimsy foundation is always going to end in a big burst bubble of tears.

I love my football. I hope West Ham finish this delayed Premier League season with a fanfare and flourish. However, the foundation of my hope for today and the future lies not in dreams that fade and die, but in the firm promise of the one who always *saves*!

For no man can lay a foundation other than the one which is laid, which is Jesus Christ.

(1 Corinthians 3 v11)

13th June: *Love is a Battlefield*

Unlike in most European and North American countries, many nations in Latin America are seeing their daily coronavirus cases and deaths spread exponentially. This means the numbers of deaths in the worst hit, Brazil, Mexico, and Peru, are doubling every two to three weeks. This led the Peruvian government's spokesperson leading their Covid-19 response to say, *'We're in bad shape. This is war'*
War can take many forms, and the fight against coronavirus, as with many battles with deadly illnesses and plagues in history, is a war on humanity. It is a war without borders against an invisible enemy. This is obviously in stark contrast to the wars between nations involving armies, tangible weapons of destruction, and the taking and defending of territory. This type of war is nowhere more epitomised than in the speech given by Winston Churchill almost exactly eighty years ago;

> *'we shall fight on the beaches,*
> *we shall fight on the landing grounds,*
> *we shall fight in the fields and in the streets,*
> *we shall fight in the hills;*
> *we shall never surrender....'*

Churchill is best remembered as the man who stood up to Hitler, eventually leading the Allies to victory in 1945. This was also a war of ideals and ideologies. The armies of fascism and democracy, with lines of battle clearly drawn on the maps of Europe. Last week Churchill became the target of Black Lives Matter protestors, his statue in Parliament Square defaced with graffiti that accused the ex-British Prime Minister of racism. Here the battle lines are not so clear, as views on Churchill's character become blurred and arguments *for* and *against* waver between historical interpretation and personal justice. Both sides of the debate provide passion, and where there is such passion and self-belief in what is right, the lines between love and hate blur as a result. Protagonists scramble to find the 'truth' with fact and opinion often merging as one.

In 1983 Pat Benatar had a hit record with *Love is a Battlefield*. Basically, the lyric focuses on the story of two people fighting to save their love. A grander interpretation, with lots of poetic licence, is that we live in a world where there is a battle for love itself. Literally, love *is* the battlefield. I am not referring to the disruption caused to our everyday existence by a deadly pandemic, yet this is a symptom of the battle. I am not talking about the sudden meteoric rise of an anti-racist movement that has opened up wounds, and galvanised cultural change. This again is a symptom of the real battle; the battle for the heart and soul of planet Earth itself.

The Bible tells us we have all openly rebelled against the Creator God. We have turned our backs on the One who first loved us. The great thing is, God has not given up on His creation! He still pours out His love to each of us every single day. He still desires for us to have a full relationship with Him. He is the same yesterday, today and forever, and His love for us will never falter. So why can we not return this love with the same unconditional nature? What stops us from opening our eyes to see the salvation that His Son Jesus Christ has won for us? That is the other great news. Jesus has already won the victory over death by dying in our place. So why do we continue to turn our backs, becoming distracted by the idols of this world?

The answer is given to us by the Apostle Paul who had his fair share of physical pain, torment, and despair as he bore witness to the living Christ 2,000 years ago.

For our struggle is not against flesh and blood, but against the rulers, against the authorities, against the powers of this dark world and against the spiritual forces of evil in the heavenly realms. (Ephesians 6 v12)

Paul says we are in a spiritual battlefield, and it not surprising therefore that with such forces working hard to separate us from the love of God, we often struggle to keep on the straight and narrow. Yet, there is more good news! God, through the power of His Holy Spirit has equipped us for the fight. With the enemy actually already defeated, we can move to the frontline with confidence, wearing the Armour of God (v13-17). In the Book of Romans, Paul writes that nothing can separate us from God's love. One of the great worship hymns of the 21st Century, *In Christ Alone*, puts this truth beautifully into words.

> *No power of hell, no scheme of man*
> *Can ever pluck me from His hand*
> *Till He returns or calls me home*
> *Here in the power of Christ I'll stand*

14th June: *On Mission*

Wycliffe Bible Translators was founded in 1953. As a result, the full Bible is now available to 700 languages and the New Testament in over 1,500 languages. However, 1.5 billion people are still without access to the full Bible. The organisation's vision of universal access is an on-going mission, and it requires the commitment and skill of the Bible translators to continue spreading the Word. The UK operation is a member of the Wycliffe Global Alliance, and currently has over 370 employees serving 530 million people speaking 360 languages in over 70 countries.

Martin and Eva are an extraordinary couple. During today's online church service, they gave us an update on their work with Wycliffe Bible Translators. Martin is currently the editor of the organisation's' prayer diary and his wife produces language maps which are used from the first stages of translation right through to engaging people with the final translated scriptures. It was Eva who introduced Martin to the work of Wycliffe after they had initially met online. Martin's dream of being an actor had not come to fruition and him, like Eva, a trained cartographer, had started to trust God that their new venture together would be their chosen calling.

They were married in 2011, and the plan was to go to work for Wycliffe where Martin would train people to bring scripture into oral cultures through working with local actors, dancers and storytellers. Eva would continue with her expertise with mapping. In 2015, as they were preparing to work and live in Thailand, Eva was sadly diagnosed with Lymphoma. For her treatment, Eva had to stay in the UK, and the couple wondered what God had in store for them next, having been so close to the calling they believed in. In his journal at the time Martin wrote, *'Where are you calling us to, Lord? Proverbs 16:9 says, "A man plans his course, but you determine his steps". I pray we see a glimmer of light...We want to do your will Lord'*

That glimmer of light came in the form of working for the Wycliffe Church Engagement Team, supporting churches in the Sheffield area. As a result, Martin was then offered the position of Prayer Diary Editor. Eva, thankfully recovering slowly from her illness continued to work in Wycliffe's mapping team from home. In practice this meant meticulously surveying places like Southeast Asia to create 'language maps' so that translation work can be targeted. Eva says, *'the maps we produce are generally considered the most authoritative language maps available, used by both Christian and secular organisations around the world.'*

In the service, Martin and Eva spoke about their continuing mission, having now travelled extensively in their current roles. God is bigger than any plan we may have in our own minds. Sometimes, we may hear the calling, see the journey, but not the path God has in *His* mind. The road to outreach and mission has not been an easy one for Martin and Eva, and yet their creative abilities have been used to touch the lives of thousands through prayer and evangelism.

Although we are not all called to the four corners of the world, God asks us all to be *on mission* for Him. This could mean being taken outside of comfort zones and going to places outside our normal social circles. In the current situation for instance, this means discussing difficult issues like racism and social injustice. It is easy to remain passive observers, often hiding behind middle class respectability. Yet, we are called not to silence, but to speak out, however uncomfortable that may feel. Coronavirus has opened up wounds and battle scars which need to be dealt with. We are reminded in Galatians 3 how we are all one in Christ. Let Martin and Eva's story help to inspire us to keep on mission.

So in Christ Jesus you are all children of God through faith, for all of you who were baptized into Christ have clothed yourselves with Christ. There is neither Jew nor Gentile, neither slave nor free, nor is there male and female, for you are all one in Christ Jesus.(v26-29)

15th June: *Retail Therapy*

After three months of a near closed economy today all the non-essential shops opened their doors. The only closed doors now belong to pubs, clubs, cafes and fast food outlets, cinemas and theatres, any place where the two metre social distancing rule cannot be implemented with the same confidence. By 7 a.m. queues formed outside the Matalans, the Primarks and the TK Maxxs around the country. Bargain hunters and those that just missed the thrill of the high street waited patiently for their turn to enter each shop of choice. Only in some of the major shopping centres in London and Birmingham were there scuffles resembling the first day of a New Year Sale.

This was shopping, but not as we have known it. Floor markings, one-way systems, closed toilet cubicles, taped off seating, contactless only payment, hand sanitisers in abundance, and face masks in congested areas. In clothes shops it is a *touch only* items you wish to buy policy, and restricted or no use changing rooms. Baskets, trolleys and surfaces are decontaminated, and items browsed but not bought put into quarantine storage. Research firm Springboard measured footfall about 40% higher than the previous week. The weather was notably warm, but numbers were still better than expected.

Another bonus for those with tooth pain is the reopening of dentists. I made an appointment to see my dentist for this afternoon and although my back molar crown had settled into a bearable twinge, the visit was welcomed. On arrival I was asked to wait outside until the one previous patient had left the building. Once inside I was asked to hand sanitise and put on a face mask. With slightly gooey hands I lifted a neatly pressed white mask from a Perspex container. I then had to answer several basic questions about coronavirus by the receptionist and my temperature was taken. Satisfied I was free from any Covid-19 symptoms I was left sitting on a plastic chair while the treatment room was being decontaminated.

Under the mask my breathing quickly became heavy and uncomfortable. Every time I exhaled my glasses steamed up. Consequently, I took them off and wiped the lenses several times. I was getting into a bit of a state when the dental nurse collected me. Dentist Ian welcomed me with his usual pleasant manner and enquired politely about the family. By this time, the sweat was gathering on my brow, I could only mumble my words, and intakes of oxygen were a visible struggle. *Think: Darth Vader having a coughing fit.* The poor dental nurse was looking bemused, and my dentist, seeing I was struggling with breath, said it was now fine to remove the mask. So I did. *Both of them*. No wonder I was gasping for air, I had taken two masks out of the container and put them on without knowing. Plonker!

The good news from the x-ray ten minutes later was the crown was still intact, with no sign of infection in the surrounding gums. After eight years, the root canal treatment was beginning to show its age, but for the moment major and very expensive treatment could wait. Check up and clean in eight weeks was arranged, when Ian the dentist said he hoped things would be back to a more simplified normal.

I would not be hurrying out to do any real retail shopping anytime soon, for a start I am not a good 'Queuer'. I applaud the patience of those who stood for hours today to enter the hallowed walls of much missed retail giants. But after my embarrassing mask incident, I was taking no chances. Sale or no sale, the Marks and Spencer Men's Department can wait.

17th June: *Food for Thought*

'Marcus Rashford, I like him!' Diana exclaimed as another picture of the Manchester United and England player was displayed on the TV screen. In fact, Diana says this every time Rashford's name is even mentioned. I am assuming it is because she appreciates the way he uses his pace to ghost past defenders and shields the ball effectively in tight spaces. Or perhaps she admires the way he keeps his cool when one-to-one with the goalkeeper, before passing the ball effortlessly into the net. No? Let's just go for, Marcus Rashford is a nice young man, who has now used his celebrity status for a good cause. Over the past week the United forward has personally lobbied the government to reverse their initial decision not to fund the free school meals programme over the Summer months.

Yesterday he got his wish with Boris and Co performing a neat Cruyff Turn (that's a U-Turn to non-football readers) and the government will now fund the £120 million it will cost to make sure 1.3 million children in England will not go hungry. These are children from low income families who are entitled to a free hot school meal during a normal term time. The pandemic has also hampered the ability of charities and community groups to add their valuable support, who often run holiday clubs to feed those who attend. Rashford, whose own mother struggled to put food on the table for her five children, has personally spearheaded a very public campaign. Andrew Forsey, from the charity Feeding Britain states,

'We owe a huge debt of gratitude to Marcus Rashford...a man who has not forgotten his roots - who is not only raising money for the cause, but has led this successful effort to help the government dig itself out of a massive hole.'

The Children's Society has now called on the government to make the free school meal extension permanent so the risk of 'holiday hunger' for our most needy young people can be virtually eradicated. Today,

Rashford has continued to put the pressure on, asking for more support for vulnerable families who struggle 'all year round'. However welcome the 'Covid summer food fund is', this has only brought us six weeks of time, he added.

Today also sees the re-start of Premier League football - along with empty stadia and fake crowd noise. I am sure when Manchester United are live on the screen, Diana will suddenly become an enthused armchair supporter of the game. After all, young Rashford is such a lovely guy who has now won the nation's hearts for the way he has conducted himself - with intelligence and sensitivity to boot! There are even tabloid headlines calling for him to be knighted. Fair play all round Sir Marcus, fair play.

19th June: *Muppet Mayhem*

Do you remember the Muppets? I grew up in the 1970s watching this crazy assortment of puppets bouncing around like demented frogs on our TV sets. Which is probably why choosing a frog to be the star made perfect sense I suppose! There have been several re-boots since their heyday which included the brilliant A Muppet's Christmas Carol with Michael Caine as Scrooge. In recent years their appeal has waned and the latest series to be aired in the US has been put on hold. One of my abiding memories of the original Muppet Show is when they all appear on screen at once in little theatre balconies, usually to sing a closing song. I remember finding this hilarious, just laughing at the pure stupidity of it. This collection of created caricatures also resembles the collective flaws in us. Kermit is the frog who cannot find love. Miss Piggy lacks social graces. Fozzie Bear is an unfunny comedian who just wants to be appreciated. Gonzo is a strange misunderstood creature no-one can relate to. Poor Beaker has not got a clue what is going on, and the mad drummer Animal...well, just speaks for himself.

What I did not realise at the time of course was that one day I would be part of an on-screen interaction of human beings that looked pretty much like frogs jumping around in boxes. Welcome to our church members online meeting. A multitude of faces in square spaces trying to replicate a 'live' church meeting using our newly acquainted friend Mr Zoom. Starting with prayer and online reflective worship led by our Pastor Graham, we soon had a series of 'catch-up monologues' from the rest of the church leadership team and a financial report. If you wished to add a prayer, give comment, or raise a question then to aid the smooth running of proceedings, you had to post in the 'chat room' first. This was because the meeting Chair could not see everyone's faces all at the same time. There were over sixty of us spread over three screens. Some folk abided by this rule, others simply forgot, which led to a myriad of anonymous voices jumping out of the screen without warning. The now familiar, *'you're on mute'* was heard at regular intervals, and when consensus was required on a decision we had to 'vote' by clicking the hand symbol. The little yellow *thumbs up* icon appeared in our face square, but disappeared after 10 seconds, so trying to count the number of affirmations was almost impossible. Fortunately, in this 'muted' atmosphere, nobody felt like rocking the virtual boat.

Credit to the meeting Chair and Graham who persevered through the disjointed communication and the technical gremlins. An intention to put us into smaller break-out rooms to discuss the impact of Covid-19 on church life was felt to be ambitious in the time remaining and we were asked to reflect on these questions outside of the meeting and give feedback as and when. These questions were:

During this period of lockdown, what do you most miss about church life? What do you not miss?

Pastor Graham was delighted with the way our church has pulled together and adapted so quickly to meeting the needs of the most vulnerable both in our own congregation and in the wider community. Praise was particular given to those responsible for delivering such a professional online presence. As a result of the Sunday Services on Zoom and other online activities throughout the week, the number of people viewing and engaging in fellowship with the church has gone from the pre-Covid hundreds to the current *thousands*. Consequently, we are now investing in a full time Technical Support worker who will continue to develop these promising outreach opportunities. As with education, it would seem that modern church life will never be the same again.

Today, we are just emerging out of strict lockdown guidelines for public places. The church building is back open for limited use - the main sanctuary now set up for thirty people to sit in socially distanced prayer rather than laid out in the normal banks of seating for over two hundred. Yet even when the restrictions are further eased allowing larger groups to congregate again, the use of technology to reach a wider audience cannot be ignored. God of course works in mysterious ways, and it should not come as a big surprise He is using this lockdown period to enrich those that know Him and touch the lives of those who are seeking. He is the God that time and time again turns Humankind's history into His Story. He has plans for us that far exceed our scope of imagination. Just when we feel the battleground is swallowing us up in fear and doubt and the picture looks bleak, God shows us His heavenly lens.

Thankfully, God does not treat us as puppets He can control in small restricted boxes, but allows us to have free will. Despite our failings and disobedience, He sees each one of our seven billion faces, and *still* loves His creation. If we sincerely endeavour to seek His face, He will give us the resources to do His will.

20th June: *Such a Big Girl!*

Everyday *Mum* and *Dad* tell me *'I'm a good girl...such a good girl'* Sometimes I know I am not so good, especially when I am tired. Then I chew things. Lately they tell me I am, *'a big girl...such a big girl'*. I am not sure what this means but I am allowed to go *walkies* off the lead in the *park*. I can go through the *gate* and up the stairs to mum and dad's *bedtime* room to see them. I can now eat *chicken and rice* for *num-nums* which is very tasty. I prefer this to *tin and biscuits*, so I ask for chicken and rice all the time now.

I saw *Donna* and she gives me a lovely wash and *groom*. I had *groom* with other dogs with *Donna* before, but this time I was on my own. I still like *groom* and I feel nice and tidy. I think *Dad* also needs *groom*. He looks not tidy and less cool. I was going to see my best friend *Fozzie* today but he is sick. *Mum* says *Fozzie* is not eating. I think *Fozzie's* mum and dad should give him *chicken and rice* and get better. I miss my best friend. To make up for this I will chase *Mo*. He likes being chased around the *kitchen* table. And around the *garden*. And around the *television* room. And around the bend.

I love playing *ball* in the *garden*. *Dad* has got me a new *ball* which I cannot chew. Bah-woof! I am good at *ball*. Dad says I'm a *clever girl* and laughs when I do something called a *Crufts turn*. I also love the *television room*. Here I sit with *mum* and *dad* on *sofa* when they are looking at nice things on *television*. They like to look at *Gardeners Worms and the Early Evening Nudes*. While they do this I chew *cushions* because I am tired. They say *'Jessica! Bad girl.'* This is confusing. If *mum* and *dad* do not want me to *chew cushions*, why are they there?

Big wag tail. I am excited. *Ball* is on *television!* My two best things together in one place. *Dad* is excited. *Dan* is excited too. *Mummy* is not so excited. When *ball* is on *television*, she is not looking at it. She is looking at a little *television* on her lap. She says *ball* is sometimes not good. She also says she likes *Mark Us Rush Foot*. I will wait nicely for this with *mum* to see if this will make *ball* good for her.

After looking at lots of *ball* with *Dad* and *Dan*, I went in *car* to see my friend Chino. *Mum* and *Dad* came in the car too. We sat in another *garden* with friends of *mum* and *dad*. They all sat on *chairs* but not together. Strange. I chased Chino around the *garden table*. Chino chased me around the *garden table*. Then we did *playtime* on the grass. *Dad* ate a lot. *Mum* talked a lot. It was late when we got *home*. I was very, very tired. *Mum* and *Dad* said I was '*such a big girl*' for playing nicely. I *am such a big girl*. I am in my *bed* now. I like being such a big girl. I *am*....such.......a............big.....Zzzz Zzzzz.

21st June: *God The Father*

This year, Sunday 21st June is both the longest day, and Father's Day. The Summer solstice should mean cloudless skies and temperatures in the high twenties. Looking out of the top bedroom window this morning it was more like a dreary February, the view marred by dark skies and heavy drizzle. It was up to Father's Day to take centre stage and live up to expectations. Not that pinning down expectations for this day is easy. For some, Father's Day is a relatively simple celebration, giving thanks for their biological father, while for others it a more complex affair. For many it is a time of sombre reflection of loss. There are those of course whose grief is very fresh as a result of Covid-19. A sensitive approach is certainly called for, and at the start of our online church service this morning, we watched a video clip that acknowledged the many types of earthly father that exist in the world today. This included recognition of the role played by stepdads, foster dads, adopted dads, granddads; and also recognition of the positive role-modelling by male youth workers, mentors and teachers.

This inclusive message is such an important one and takes on even greater significance during this time of personal reflection and community soul searching. The role of the father figure in whatever social context that may be is as vital as ever. I am blessed to have two young people in my life now that have been a credit to their mum, and who I can call my friends as well as my stepchildren. The transition to our new family group has not been plain sailing these past six years, and welcoming me into their lives, along with my natural children has required a great deal of patience and understanding. Their stepdad card sits pride of place alongside my Daniel's, and one from Jess the Cockerpoo. The day is also touched with sadness that my 23-year-old daughter remains distant in both miles and emotional connectivity. This is a reconciliation that God willing, will have to wait for another day.

My daughter's absence is a reminder of our fallibilities and humanity. Father's Day can bring with it the hurt of broken relationships, as well as the joy of togetherness. It is for this reason that as Christians we can also focus on the Fatherhood of God. Our online meeting was full of pre-recorded personal testimonies of those who bear witness to the uniqueness of God as our heavenly Father. Even the most cherished Earthly fathers suffer from human frailty, sometimes through unintended mishap, sometimes through deliberate hurtful action. God the Father provides us with the ultimate template for unconditional love. To those who seek to know Him, He is forever faithful to us and more than makes up for our human shortcomings.

The Bible teems with references to God being the Creator and Father of humanity. It is one of the key themes of the Christian faith and should not be under-estimated nor over-looked.

Yet for us there is one God, the Father, from whom are all things and for whom we exist
1 Corinthians 8 v6

And I will be a father to you, and you shall be sons and daughters to me, says the Lord Almighty
2 Corinthians 6 v18

One God and Father of all, who is over all and through all and in all.
Ephesians 4 v6

But the good news does not stop there! The character of God the Father extends to all. It is an inclusive deal. Why? Because Jesus the Son died to make it inclusive! The invitation extends to each one of us, whatever the past has 'slaved' us in. The service reading today was taken from Psalm 68, a reminder of God's fully inclusive love for His children.

"Father of the fatherless and protector of the widows is God in his holy habitation." Psalm 68 v5

In the complexities of our emotions and insecurities of our feelings we can be secure in the Father who is forever patient; whose kindness never runs out; who is always approachable; you will never have to earn

His love; you will never muck it up enough for Him not to love you; He always has the very best for you in mind; He will protect you with his perfectly timed discipline. His Fatherly wisdom and generosity know no bounds.

In a pre-recorded testimony for the service, I was thankful to still have my earthly father as a good spiritual role model to call upon. As for my heavenly Father? I acknowledged He is simply the One who knows me better than I know myself.

23rd June: *Bird's Eye View*

Mr Pigeon: Did you see the final Government Briefing on the TV earlier Muriel?

Mrs Pigeon: No Cedric, of course not, I was feeding the twins. You know how hungry they get. Double worms and bird seed from the swinging thingy. Happy feathers.

Mr P: Well, anyway I watched it through their window as usual. It was the human with the large flop of hair again. Difficult to lip read because he mumbles, but I got the gist of it. It is all changing on the 4th July!

Mrs P: Two Slugs Cedric?

Mr P: Thank you dear. Pass the dirt powder please. My favourite, you do spoil me Muriel. Boys, keep the noise down...you'll have the Magpies complaining again.

Twins: Sorry Dad! We'll fly over to Perry's and play poop the deck at No 17.

Mrs P: You boys! Don't be late. Sorry, you were saying Cedric?

Mr P: It all changes on July 4th my *flutterfly*. People can now move closer together if it is not possible to keep to the two metres. At one metre they still need to observe precautions to reduce the risk of transmission.

Mrs P: Your lip reading is so much better since the lockdown my love. Carry on.

Mr P: Well, all businesses are being asked to help people make common sense decisions.

Mrs P: That old hazelnut eh? *Human common sense.*

Mr P: The big news... is restaurants, pubs and cafes can reopen, with limited contact between staff and customers. Except customers have to *give* their contact details when they enter.

Mrs P: How bizarre. At least we can get back to good honest scavenging in pub gardens.

Mr P: Good point Muriel. The Twins will love playing the table-hopping game! Anyway, there is more. Holiday accommodation can also re-open and people can stay away from their home again. But they cannot use shared toilets.

Mrs P: Perish the thought. They should try sharing this nest! Anything else re-opening dear?

Mr P: Yes. museums, cinemas, playgrounds and hairdressers. The Paul person will be pleased with that. Have you seen what sits on the top of his head these days? I am tempted to drop one on it.

Mrs P: Now behave Cedric. The family of people have fed us well since our arrival in Spring. All that lovely bread. I do believe that was the remains of a Marks and Spencer white tin we enjoyed yesterday.

Mr P: Sorry Muriel, wash my beak out! So, the last bit of the Briefing explained the new rules for meeting up. Two households can now meet indoors, two metres apart still, though they can stay the night. All a bit confusing.

Mrs P: Nightclubs and theatres?

Mr P: No, not yet. That will be disappointing for our London cousins. They have so missed their weekend food binge.

Mrs P: And what are the new numbers? – that is the important bit. Did you get those Cedric?

Mr P: 'Moving in the right direction' flop head said. The seven day average trend for both new cases and Covid-19 related deaths are as low as they were pre-lockdown.

Mrs P: That is good for the people. We will be seeing even more of them out and about now.

Mr P: Even more not abiding by the rules you mean! We have seen the heavy traffic in the mornings along the road behind us my fluff-bundle...guess it is back to normal from now on. *Oh no!* Here comes trouble...

Mrs P: The cockerpoo out for her evening rant! Barking at all and sundry to assert her dominance. The twins are safely down the road. Let's play our favourite game!

Mr P: Good idea Muriel. We just fly over to the extension roof and sit there like stuffed....pigeons. It drives the dog barmy. Hilarious! This time can I do the long continuous hard stare at her?

Mrs P: Of course you can *plumpy*, you deserve to after watching all 92 daily briefings through the window. Quick, to the roof!

24th June: *A Stitch in Time*

'She's done it!' I shouted, punching the air and leaping off the sofa as if West Ham had scored a late winner to escape relegation. 'She so deserved to win', added Diana who was equally pleased with the verdict of the Great British Sewing Bee judges. Our favourite contestant, and the one who I had picked out from week two as the dark horse of the competition, had won a tense final. A victory sealed through the creation of a classy but understated 'red carpet' dress in the last *made to measure* challenge. It could not have happened to a more apt person as we all tentatively emerge out of lockdown.

At the end of the programme viewers were told that since being crowned unofficial amateur champion, medical consultant Clare Bradley has had little time to continue her meticulous approach to sewing. Like many NHS consultants specialising in other areas, she has been called upon to help on the coronavirus front line. It was clear from watching the series, which had been filmed before the Covid crises, that Clare's patience, attention to detail and ability to work under pressure often set her apart from the other contestants.

Clare's story was a reminder that despite daily messages of 'we are heading in the right direction' from government ministers, NHS teams across the country are still caring for hundreds of people in our hospitals who are fighting for their lives on ventilators. However, this week we have had positive reviews from coronavirus vaccine centres that trials are going well. Alok Sharma, the Business Secretary, said that the clinical trial at the University of Oxford was progressing well and, if successful, doses could be ready by the end of Summer. Live human trials are accelerating too, but both scientists and medical advisors continue also to give the caveat, 'this process could take several more months' and even then 'a fully effective vaccine may never be found'. The race against time to vaccinate the seven billion people on planet earth continues at haste.

In some ways the past three months have flown by, with one day just flowing almost unnoticed into the next. In other ways it has been a series of Deja vu moments as if time has stood still. Perhaps it is the overload of numbers and government directives on the brain that has numbed us. Very George Orwell. The statistics remain grim reading in the UK. With over 42,000 recorded coronavirus deaths, we are third in the World behind The USA and now Brazil. The promised test and trace app has now been put on hold due to technical issues. Lockdown easing has enabled many to go back to work or see loved ones again, though scenes of crowded sun-kissed beaches, busy highways and by-ways, and concerns that social distancing adherence is becoming an exception rather than the rule point to tricky days ahead. Yet in terms of where we are compared to other nations, it could be argued we have escaped an even harsher Covid reality.

As of 24th June, there are now over nine million confirmed cases across 188 countries, with a reported 500,000 lives being lost. Among the worst affected in recent weeks, Brazil, Chile, Mexico and Ecuador have seen vicious widespread outbreaks. The World Health Organisation reports the pandemic has not reached its peak in Central and South America. Brazil is regularly recording more than 1,000 deaths a day with the total death toll now around 55,000. Furthermore, small second waves are being seen in China, Iran, Portugal, parts of the USA and even in Germany which has suffered sharp regional spikes after a relatively successful first wave response.

The impact on the home economy has moved from 'worrying prediction' to 'harsh reality' level. By midnight on 14 June 2020, 9.1 million employees have been furloughed through the Government's Coronavirus Job Retention Scheme (CJRS). This includes 59% of the employees in the accommodation and food services sector, 48% of the employees in the arts, entertainment, recreation and other services sector, and 46% of the employees in the construction sector. 2.8 million people claimed unemployment related benefits by May. The number of people who will lose their jobs after the furlough schemes ends after the Summer is a real concern. The large numbers of redundancies are already coming through. Rolls Royce, Centrica and Swissport have announced drastic cuts in their workforce. Today, the huge shopping centre giant Intu has collapsed into administration.

In the Post 16 Education and Training sector we are bracing ourselves for an influx of young people whose apprenticeship scheme has collapsed, as well as an expected high demand from adults who have lost their job and need re-skilling. Through luck rather than by design, the introduction of a new Adult Digital Skills offer is almost ready to launch. One consequence of the pandemic is how fast colleges and other training providers have adapted to the need to deliver remote online learning. According to the Association of Colleges, the sector has apparently advanced digital learning provision quicker in the past three months than in the previous five years. The battlefield of war has always had a morbid relationship with scientific advancement and technological progress.

For those of us who are basically confined to their homes in lockdown, there have been weekly events which have given the weeks structure and routine. For Diana and I it has been the sanctuary of the garden, the Sunday online service, the walks with Jess 'around the block' and must-watch programmes like The Great British Sewing Bee. That was our Wednesday evening go-to TV. Now it has ended, it leaves a gap in the schedule. Not to worry, football is back, and Dan has just treated himself to a three-month Sky Sports package. This means wall to wall Premier League is now possible. Sewing Bee replaced by football on tap? Diana may feel she has just been stitched up!

26th June: *30 Years of Hurt*

Liverpool FC are celebrating their first Premier League title, and their first top-flight domestic league title for thirty years. Those of us who grew up in the 70s and 80s watching the Anfield club win domestic and European titles on a regular basis, it seemed totally implausible to think it would take so long before such a triumph occurred again. It was interesting to look up what was in the news in 1990. It was the year of German Reunification; the launch of the Hubble Telescope; and Tim Berners-Lee invented the World Wide Web. In the UK, the Poll Tax riots led to the resignation of Margaret Thatcher with John Major chosen to take up the helm. The big winners at the cinema included Home Alone, Ghost, Pretty Woman and the unforgettable Teenage Mutant Ninja Turtles. In the music charts Tears for Fears, The Red Hot Chilli Peppers and the Minogue sisters Kylie and Dannii were strutting their stuff. While The Fresh Prince of Bel-Air, Cheers and Beverley Hills 90210 were US imports invading our living rooms. We were also introduced to a family from Springfield called The Simpsons.

In sport, Kenny Dalglish's Liverpool won the then First Division, The Commonwealth Games were held in Auckland, and Mike Tyson ruled the boxing world. Perhaps the defining image of the sporting year though was Paul Gascoigne in tears knowing he would miss the World Cup Final in Rome. Of course, England succumbed to the Germans in *that* penalty shoot-out, and the rest as we say, is history.

How time and the mind conspire to plays tricks. The memory of Chris Waddle blasting the ball over the bar in Turin, and the feeling which followed seem like yesterday. Yet, the site of the Berlin Wall coming down in November 1989 seems like three lifetimes ago. Perhaps it is the emotional connection that prints itself in the memory, making the event more personal, and therefore leaving the lasting impression. If that is the case, how will we remember 2020? For Liverpool fans, especially those not even born in 1990, the celebrations last night in the city were an explosion of sheer delight and a sense of relief knowing the wait was finally over. The lockdown suspension of the Premier League would certainly have increased the anxiety - there was even speculation the football season would be null and void if the pandemic could not be tamed in time. For those who have lost loved ones as a direct result of Covid-19, 2020 would simply be a painful memory, perhaps for the remainder of their own lives. For those families who God willing have been spared the worst-case scenario, there are likely to be a range of emotions and memories from this unprecedented time.

For me, it is the slowdown of pace. It is the way each one of us has responded to the hiatus, as many normal routines evaporated overnight in March. The absence of the office, the classroom, the university lecture theatre, the radio studio, the weekly shop, the family gathering, the drink with neighbours, the visit to a National Trust Property, the eat out treat, the cinema popcorn; all replaced by enforced physical confinement. In turn this has led to more time, to awake, to ponder, to reflect, to grasp, to self-challenge, to value, to consider options, to sit, to talk, to evaluate, to recognise, to assimilate, to create, to re-design, to re-invent. To learn patience, to seek wisdom, to be thankful, to love with less conditions, to find comfort in the detail, to appreciate the simplicity, to share goodness, to share the lows, to enjoy the silence, to re-connect, and to wait on His presence.

Be still and know I am God

In thirty years' time, my hope is when people look back at 2020 they see a time of opportunity not pain. They see humanity at its best, not at its worst. They see a re-birth of togetherness, of mutual appreciation and respect. They see a revival of faith over fear. The history books will say, in a time of great uncertainty and adverslty, the world reconnected with itself, and in doing so reconnected with the Heavenly Father.

27th June: *On a Knife Edge*

In times of a National Security crises or a terrorist incident the Prime Minister calls upon the COBRA (Cabinet Office Briefing Rooms) Committee. The rather less threatening sounding SAGE (Scientific Advisory Group for Emergencies) has been the mainstay authority on all things Covid-19. One of its members, Sir Jeremy Farrar today announced the UK remains 'on a knife edge' and he is worried about a surge in cases ahead of pubs and restaurants opening on 4th July. Sir Jeremy warned there could be a 'very nasty rebound' leading up to the Winter if cases increased over the months ahead. There have been grave concerns expressed by other scientists and medical professionals over recent illegal street parties taking place, coupled with the sight of thousands heading for the beaches in the hot weather. The West Midlands police and crime commissioner criticised the decision to reopen pubs in England on a Saturday with pent up demand likely to see alcohol spilling out into the streets. Meanwhile the Home Secretary, Priti Patel is considering the first city-based lock down being imposed in Leicester after several hundred cases were recorded in just two weeks.

Today we travelled to Reading to help Sarah clear out her room, situated on the third floor of a student rented townhouse: the one we rescued her from the day after lockdown started. The original plan was for Sarah to leave her romantic social bubble in East London with Owen and go straight back to live in this house, until the tenancy expired at the end of June. Last weekend a man with a history of mental illness walked into a park near this Reading townhouse and stabbed three men to death. With the area cordoned off and the incident raw in the headlines, and in our heads, it was agreed that Sarah came back to Redhill instead.

This was another knife crime killing that has come to plague our country in recent years. Yes, this was not a gang related incident, and the victims were not city teenagers in the wrong place at the wrong time, but the *knife* has become the convenient weapon of choice. Easy to get hold of, and easy to dispose of, the knife has almost become the national symbol of violence. Earlier this month two women were stabbed to death in a

North-West London park. Two days ago, a policeman survived a knife attack in a Glasgow hotel. At the end of 2019, the number of offences in the UK involving knives rose by 7% to over 45,000 in the year.

Life is fragile. The three friends in that Reading park were enjoying the early evening warmth, chatting and laughing together after months of social distancing. Within moments, the random act of a stranger led to an ending of life that is in every sense a tragedy. It is a singular horror story in the middle of a larger dark global narrative. The world also remains on a knife edge as Covid-19 claims its 500,000th official victim, with 10 million cases of contagion recorded. The situation in South America and India has gone past that edge. With little Government direction or support, health care systems crumble under the demand for beds. It is all relative, but again the most vulnerable in society are bearing the brunt. With the very poorest trapped in overcrowded housing hubs, we must not forget our human brothers and sisters unable to escape the ravages of the disease. At home, we are concerned about irresponsible behaviours and potential disorder outside pubs. In Brazil and India there is no edge to cling on to. There is just a precipice into which the Worlds Health Authority has predicted these nations will fall into.

29th June: Patient 91

In the UK, we are now 100 days into the lockdown period. In this time, there have been many examples of bravery, fortitude and battles against the odds. Yet there is one story which has come to our attention this week of a man whose plight has been so extraordinary that I just need to share it. I also would like to credit the reporting of this story to Oliver Barnes and Bui Thu - an amazing piece of journalism.

Scottish pilot, 42-year-old Stephen Cameron spent 68 days on a ventilator, the longest stretch recorded to date, and survived. However, he did not do this in a hospital in his hometown of Motherwell, but in Ho Chi Minh City, thousands of miles from friends and family, in Vietnam. Home to 95 million people this story starts with the remarkable fact Vietnam has only seen a few hundred cases of coronavirus, and not a single recorded death. With such a record to defend, the case of Stephen Cameron, the sickest patient the Vietnamese medical teams had to deal with since the outbreak, soon became a national story, his road to recovery detailed in newspapers and news bulletins. After he fell ill in March, public health officials gave him the reference, Patient 91 - and this number has been etched into the public's imagination up to this day.

As with many Western pilots, Cameron headed for Asia to find work in the healthy regional air travel industry. Before he was due to take control of his first flight, he visited an expat bar to meet a friend, the night before Ho Chi Minh City was due to shut down. The Buddha Bar and Grill was packed with St Patrick Day revellers, but Cameron and his friend played pool, kept themselves to themselves and went home. After his maiden flight, a fever developed and along with 12 others who had been at the same bar, Cameron tested positive. It was the single biggest outbreak in south Vietnam and initially there was little sympathy for the foreigner. Patient 91 soon became the scapegoat for the incident. In response the authorities linked 4,000 people to the outbreak, were quickly tested, and a strict quarantine followed.

On March 18, Cameron was admitted to hospital, but quickly deteriorated as his lungs, kidneys, liver, and blood flow lost function. Plugged into an Ecmo machine, used for the most seriously ill Covid patients, Cameron spent ten weeks in an induced coma. One of his friends was told by the Foreign office there was a 10% chance of recovery and he sold Cameron's apartment in morbid anticipation. Whilst the medical teams attended to the Scotsman, all the other ICU patients in the hospital recovered and were discharged. The death rate of zero and the fate of Stephen Cameron became inextricably linked. Politicians started to visit the hospital, and the public, once scorning of the visitor from the West, began to root for his survival. Whatever they did, it worked.

When doctors woke him up on 12 June, Cameron soon realised how much the world had changed. Globally, seven times more had contracted the disease than when he entered his coma. Yet, Vietnam has seemingly remained relatively unscathed, with few serious transmissions and no lives lost. Part perhaps due to the early diligence of the government, part due to the way in which the public took the virus seriously from day one and obeyed the lockdown rules.

The turnaround in Cameron's health had been down to the sheer determination of medical staff to keep their miraculous record intact. "If I'd been almost anywhere else on the planet, I'd be dead. They would have flicked the switch after 30 days," he declared from his hospital bed. Now undertaking physiotherapy to help bring back the strength in his legs, Stephen Cameron is looking forward to returning home. A flight has been booked for 12 July, but as with many national incidents, things have become very political. In particular, the question of who is going to foot the bill is still ongoing. At approximately £5,000 a day to operate, just the use of the Ecmo machine itself illustrates how the cost of treatment can spiral out of control. Insurers, the British Embassy and the Vietnamese regional government have a bit of negotiating to do.

The politics of his return are a reminder that the miraculous recovery of Patient 91 is not just a story of a Scottish pilot who recovered from

Covid-19 and overcame the odds. It is the story of how a developing Southeast Asian country with a turbulent recent history beat the odds too. I look forward to the making of the movie.

30th June: *Schools of Thought*

Another long day at the laptop. As the teaching and learning lead at the local college the end of each academic year brings in an increased workload. This is traditionally the time in Further Education for professional development activity for both teaching teams and support staff. Normally this means planning for several days of training that meets both the strategic requirements of the college, and the differentiated needs of its workforce. However, what is meaningful and worthwhile 'CPD' for plumbing lecturers can be vastly different to that of a group of art and design practitioners. You then have those teaching additional and high needs students, those delivering courses at Higher Education level, and those offering technical provision for apprentices. Quite a mixed bag, and to keep all happy, on board and moving along in roughly the same direction is a challenge.

Of course, this year, it's a whole new ball game. For a start, we still have students coming onto the campus completing practical assessments, even though most can progress onto next year through a combination of finished coursework and predicted achievement. The vast majority of teaching staff remain working from home like me, and the feeling of isolation and disempowerment will have taken its toll. Despite keeping the fire burning with online resources, links to webinars, and sharing good practice on e-platforms, only half of the workforce had visibly engaged in *corporate identity activity*.

So all in all, end of year staff training was tricky. Reflections of teaching in lockdown, *yes can do*, and what we have learnt about student learning behaviours, *yes can do*, but thinking about what the new academic year would look like was a stab in the dark. Government guidelines had switched to a more flexible 'do what you can with social distancing' and 'prepare for local lockdowns if needed', but plans to bring back all pupils and students after the Summer has become a high stakes political game.

There is always less policy focus on Further Education - often regarded as the Cinderella of the education world - so the new instruction for schools is to keep pupils in *class bubbles,* and to reduce the risk of infection. Sounds reasonable, and for nursery and primary provision, feasible. But for secondary schools and colleges where learners move from subject to subject made up of bespoke learning groups, this is impractical. So two 'schools of thought' have emerged. The first, that it will be 'life as normal' by September and this is all much ado about nothing. The second; planning should centre on the worst case scenario and fingers and thumbs are all crossed that a combined face to face and online delivery package will work itself out.

My college leadership team had opted for both, and...neither. Timetables would run as normal, but the learner cohort would be split in two. Half of the students would therefore be in one week, the other half in the week after; rotating between face to face and independent online learning. It was a comfort first approach, and if we returned to 'normal' this would be perceived as a good move. If not, then its high risk, with students asked to stay at home for a week at a time after spending the best part of six months doing exactly that. Not a great transition back to learning.

Yesterday I visited the campus for the first time so my ailing laptop could have an MOT. I knew the main building would be heralded with instruction posters, arrows, sanitisers and Perspex screens. Yet, it was the complexity of the newly signed 'one way' system that baffled and bewildered. My first attempt at reaching the third floor IT support zone ended in a dead end. I reversed and tried route two, this time taking a circuitous route through the Resource Centre, up a back stairwell and meandering across an open planned office space to find my targeted destination. I decided not to try and find my office in case I got lost between the Reprographics room and the photocopier outside room A101.

Time will tell of course as to what exactly awaits schools and colleges in September. With the prospect of *second waves* and *local spikes* the uncertainty in planning for learning could be with us well into the next academic year. To be honest, I am just happy not to be a parent with school age children, a teacher responsible for very young pupils, or a Headteacher/Principal making the ultimate call. I will keep plugging away at supporting teachers at my own college, and whatever the future brings, maintain a smile and give a comforting word. The one thing all in education agree with - that the effect of this long lockdown on learners, teachers, support staff and leaders has had an unprecedented impact on mental health and well-being. For many this will not be apparent until the entrance doors open again in September.

JULY 2020

1st July: *Divided Loyalties*

Pinch and a punch, first day of the month, and no returns. This odd phrase originated either from an Olde English tradition for dealing with witches (a pinch of salt to make them weak followed by a firm punch in the *cauldron* apparently); or from when President George Washington provided local Indian tribes with fruit punch and an added pinch of salt. What a lot of nonsense! The saying obviously comes from a C20th tradition for following your football team when they are going through bad times. It involves an action at the start of every month where you have to pinch and punch yourself as a reminder that you support a team that promises hope, but often under-delivers. It is an unwritten rule of thumb - the commitment, passion and emotional investment you put into your football team is rarely matched by a return on that investment.

This season has just been like that, with both my football teams having a bit of a 'mare. The club I grew up with in the 1980s has become a bit of an embarrassment. There has been no 'it's nice to be beside the seaside' for Southend Utd. The Essex Blues won only four league matches in the shortened season, and with League One Chairmen voting to end the campaign without another ball being kicked, it is down to the fourth tier of the English professional league for next season. Even before the pandemic, the club were in financial disarray with players not being paid on time, and tax bills unpaid. On the pitch former England defender Sol Campbell had been chosen last September to stop the rot in form, which started early last season when the club missed relegation by the skin of their teeth in the 19/20 campaign. Last week Campbell left by mutual consent. Several players have already departed to save money. The future looks bleak.

As you know my 'family club' is West Ham United who despite having a decent playing squad on paper, were sitting precariously close to the Premier League drop zone. Unlike the lower leagues, the Premier League will now be completing all domestic fixtures, but behind closed doors. Tonight, the Hammers were at home to Chelsea, a team supported by son and stepson: and both teams needed three points badly, Chelsea looking upwards rather than down with a highly prized Champions League place in their sights. Live on Sky, the match kick-off at 8.15 pm was a greatly anticipated affair.

'Don't forget we have our Church Growth Group at 8 pm later', Diana called from the kitchen. *Aaah, so we do*, I mused to myself. There might have to be a compromise here, and I was OK in missing the opening 30 mins of the match. We would hold the Zoom meeting in the kitchen, the boys watching the game in the lounge. They would let me know if any goals were scored. It was a plan. God would understand - in fact, my actions will be rewarded with a West Ham win!

After a social chat with our Church friends, we read Psalm 6 and reflected on the words of King David. I have come to appreciate how The Book of Psalms in the Old Testament has provided a connection to our present day situation. In many of them David is in dire straits! Often surrounded by the enemies of Israel and betrayed by those closer to the throne, he turns to God for deliverance. Psalm 6 starts in this manner - it is a cry from the heart of a man who wears his emotions loudly on his royal sleeves:

> Lord, do not rebuke me in your anger
> or discipline me in your wrath.
>
> Have mercy on me, Lord, for I am faint;
> heal me, Lord, for my bones are in agony.

> My soul is in deep anguish.
> How long, Lord, how long?
> Turn, Lord, and deliver me;
>
> save me because of your unfailing love.
>
> Among the dead no one proclaims your name.
> Who praises you from the grave?
> I am worn out from my groaning.
>
> All night long I flood my bed with weeping
> and drench my couch with tears.
>
> My eyes grow weak with sorrow;
> they fail because of all my foes.

This is prayer of desperation, for David knows he cannot rely on his own strength. He even tries to negotiate with God: *please do not let me die, how can I praise you if I'm dead!* How human is that! However, these groans of pain are not the end of the passage. David suddenly becomes resurgent in faith. Why? Because he knows his God listens and acts.

> Away from me, all you who do evil,
> for the Lord has heard my weeping.
>
> The Lord has heard my cry for mercy;
> the Lord accepts my prayer.
>
> All my enemies will be overwhelmed with shame and anguish;
> they will turn back and suddenly be put to shame.

David ends on a positive, at ease knowing his prayer is heard. That in itself is comforting. He also has faith in the God who took him from being a simple shepherd boy to the King of a chosen nation. He knows this faith will ultimately lead to victory over those who conspire against him. So, our small group closed in prayer, thinking of those who faced daily adversity and hardship. In such dark valleys we believe the light of hope shines through Christ, who came to fulfil the promises God, the same promises made to David several centuries earlier.

I then joined the boys in the lounge. Much to my surprise, West Ham were putting up a fight against Chelsea's superior team. An entertaining match ensued, the near empty London Stadium not influencing the intensity of the play, the position of both teams in the League being motivation enough. We arrived at time added on, the score 2-2, and a point apiece seemed on the cards. An honourable draw we think, sitting on the edge of our sofa cushions. Then West Ham counterattack, the ball finding Andriy Yarmolenko who lashes it sweetly past the Chelsea keeper. Gooooaaaalllll...against the odds the Premier League strugglers score a late winner. The boys folded their arms in disgust as I leapt around the room like a demented wallaby. I could *pinch* myself...and *punch* the air. Rarely in the context of this current season, one of my teams had returned on my emotional investment!

I then acknowledged the need to put the same emotional investment into a God who always listens; who has always been the Father who loves me without condition. A God who always provides a return on my emotional investment, especially when I least expect. I am sure West Ham still would have won this evening, even if I had skipped Growth Group to watch the whole match. But then I would not have learnt a little more about the power of prayer.
Last minute winner! God does move in very mysterious ways.

3rd July: *Unchained Melody*

The countdown has started in England. Tomorrow, the pubs and restaurants are back open and the pent-up public will be unleashed onto the high streets. Everyone has been told to behave, business owners have been reminded about their obligations to keep their clients safe and in check, and the police are waiting in the wings to see if their services are required. Local Reigate High Street is preparing itself for the revelries, shutting off traffic tonight so additional signage and zonal markings can be put in place. All the country waits with bated breath, except for poor Leicester - the only place locked down for a further two weeks due to a large spike in Covid-19 cases.

I can safely say a visit to the pub is not on our agenda. Diana and I are virtually teetotal these days and a table at one of our favourite eating establishments is more likely in the next week or so. For now, a Friday when neither of us are working is an opportunity to revisit parts of the garden where the recent rain has not reached. Shrubs not flowering are moved to sunnier spots, patches of turf Jess has used as peeing points are attended to, and the netted allotment is harvested for a forest of lettuce.

The other *home* news is the arrival this afternoon of *quizmeister*, Owen who is staying over the weekend to see Sarah, as she is celebrating her 20th birthday on Sunday. So early afternoon I took Sarah to Redhill station to pick up Owen, a short drive from where we live. Pulling into the station carpark I noticed my college line manager Rebecca standing with face mask on looking very perplexed. She was staring despondently at the large station bicycle rack in front of her. I wound the window down and joked, 'lost your bike?' - I knew Rebecca rode from the station to the college, but it also dawned on me - *why was she going to the college on a closure day?* Sadly, my throwaway question was too close for comfort. Someone had cut through the padlock and stolen Rebecca's bike. She was travelling into work to carry out staff recruitment interviews, and now she was wheelless and stranded. Owen had not yet arrived on the London Bridge train, so Sarah agreed to wait on while I offered to take Rebecca to the college.

Still understandably quite distraught at the loss of her bike, Rebecca climbed into the front passenger seat. We have, I hope she would agree, an effective working relationship. Both relatively new to the college, and both agreeing approaches on how to improve the day to day experiences of teachers and students. I was pleased to have been in the right place at the right time to help out. It was pure coincidence meeting at the station that led to an opportunity to show some kindness. Or was it? You never know with God. He has an unerring tendency to put us in times and places which do not always logically add up. Well, in our human understanding of *logic* that is.

Over the years I have learnt to just roll with it, not to ask or question, and let be what will be. The benefits work both ways. I have often met someone unexpectantly, who has then offered me a word of encouragement or an act of kindness that has in turn influenced me for the better. *Kindness* is not monopolised by Christians of course, nor should it be. What we are charged to do though is share the source and inspiration of our endeavours. This is the challenge of a faith centred life. In this instance, the practical act in giving a colleague a lift mattered to the recipient; and the hope is this in turn might offer a further opportunity to witness in the future. Yet we so often fall short in sharing the words which could make the difference to others. Maybe it is an English trait to keep things uncomplicated, neat and tidy. *We don't want to cause offence.* Political correctness has arguably made us over-wary of upsetting both friends and strangers.

As such we often lack the courage of our convictions and the opportunity slips by. Fortunately, our oversight however, becomes God's *over sight*. We might not always see the bigger picture, but God has a firm handle on the past, the present and the future. He is the Bible tells us in so many way, the same yesterday, today and forever. In an unchained, unhinged, and fragmented world God sees every link in the cycle of life He created. Sometimes our chain falls off, but God is there to give us a lift to set us on our way again. That is the Good News we must share.

4th July: *Inn Dependence Day*

Very wisely, the government instructed pubs not to open until 6 a.m. this morning rather than one minute past midnight. Inevitably there were still queues of punters outside the Dog and Duck and the Gherkin and Ferret in every high street (except in Leicester), country lane and village green. On the whole, mass anarchy did not materialise, but the chair of the Police Federation, John Apter, pointed to the rather obvious assertion that 'it was crystal clear drunk people and social distancing don't mix'. The media supported this by showing a catalogue of images; streets full of drinkers in close proximity, enjoying the chance to congregate once again. Apter noted there was still the usual combination of 'naked men, happy drunks, angry drunks...and more angry drunks', but overall, the NHS reported a quiet day and there were relatively few arrests across the country.

If going for that pint was not your cup of tea, then 'Super Saturday' offered a wider range of lockdown easing alternatives. Hairdressers and barber shops welcomed long haired natives, saving the day for those who had self-styled once too often. Most salons went for pre-booking only, with appointment times going faster than Glastonbury tickets. Bingo halls, museums and galleries opened their doors once again, and cinema visits were back, but with drastically reduced capacity per screening. Strangely though, theatres remain closed, possibly due to the risk to on-stage performers rather than risk to the spread-out audience. One person monologues and stand-up comedy could become very popular! Joking apart, the impact on jobs and careers in the live entertainment sector is not a laughing matter. Indoor gyms and fitness centres also remain closed and are taking a huge financial hit.

Funfairs and theme parks can welcome customers with high volume sanitising and strictly managed ride queues. Churches and other religious buildings can accommodate small numbers for prayer and worship, and therefore weddings with very select guest lists can also go ahead. Having been through the process of matrimony planning twice, I would not fancy trying to cut down the family and friends' guest-list to the post-lockdown allowed *thirty*. However, this does represent a good reason perhaps to exclude grumpy Great-aunt Maud, or the ever-embarrassing Uncle Ernie from the celebrations.

So the balance lines between the state of the nation's economic health and it's mental well-being have been drawn. The case of Leicester is a current reminder how the balance can quickly shift. The scientists, politicians and the statisticians are now focusing on the spikes and the blips. Abroad, the blips have already begun. Melbourne in Australia for example has just locked itself down again. As mentioned before, many US states are wavering on that knife-edge. England's own Chief Medical officer, the now household name of Prof Chris Whitty, remains cautious in his assessment. Lockdown easing, he says, is far from 'risk free'. Covid-19 is still very much with us.

A further 200 people died in the last 48 hours after testing positive for coronavirus, bringing the death toll in the UK to 44,220.

5th July: *Audacious Hope*

In our church online service this morning Pastor Graham challenged the listening congregation with a question. *On meeting others, what do you talk about in the first thirty minutes?* The premise being what we choose to talk about tells others a lot about where our interests and passions lie. For Graham, he confessed, it was his love of all things cycling which usually made an early appearance in conversation. It is human nature to try and communicate what we feel makes us...well *us*. As well as our hobbies and interests - which for many men seem to gravitate around a passion for sport - the other two topics which tend to dominate are *work* and *family*. It is these things that define us, and many of us feel comfortable in readily sharing what we are *'in to'*. It is natural to seek common ground which then helps to develop our social inter-connections. If we find enough connections with that 'other' then there is the foundation to take the relationship further.

For example, two of our newest friends are the owners of Fozzie, another Cockerpoo whom Jess has grown up with, ever since they first met at puppy socialisation classes last year. The common thread therefore being the dogs, and our human friendship has grown out of that. More often than not connections are made simply because the two parties involved belong to the same generation, experiencing the same issues and challenges, sharing experiences from the same life cycle stage. So, young couples with babies tend to gravitate towards each other, and older 'empty nesters' often do the same. Graham's question of course was to make us reflect on *where, when, and how* we share our Christian faith with others. My mind cast back to the bike incident on Friday.

The service Bible reading was taken from Acts Chapter 8: 26-40. In the passage an early church evangelist called Philip was sent by the other disciples to minister in Samaria. In this land Philip experienced much success in bringing people to faith, healing the sick and baptising in the name of Christ. One day, an angel of the Lord told Philip to travel further south to a road between Jerusalem and Gaza. There he met a eunuch, an important official who was treasurer for Candace, queen of Ethiopia. The official was on his way back from worshipping at the Jewish temple in Jerusalem, and when Philip encountered him, he was sitting in his chariot, reading aloud from a scroll.

"He was led like a sheep to the slaughter, and as a lamb before the shearer is silent, so he did not open his mouth. In his humiliation he was deprived of justice. Who can speak of his descendants? For his life was taken from the earth." Isaiah 53 v7

The Ethiopian did not understand who the Old Testament prophet Isaiah was speaking about. As a eunuch, he also knew he could not be accepted into the Jewish tradition. He was a man seeking to know more, and Philip immediately explained the story of Jesus, and God's plan of salvation. The message was a powerful one to this willing and open listener, and straight away the official asked to be baptised as a believer. A pool of water was nearby, and Philip gladly baptised him there and then in the middle of the hot desert. After this Philip was led away by the Spirit leaving the queen's treasurer to continue his journey home. The result of this encounter is unknown, but historical records show that soon afterwards, the Christian faith spread within the Ethiopian region, and then gradually outwards to other parts of Africa.

Philip was full of passion. He could not stop telling others about *that* passion. What this story also shows is how God will direct us to the very margins of society towards those who are seeking His Name. The Ethiopian would not have been accepted under the laws of Judaism and may have considered himself unworthy of acceptance as an outsider and a eunuch. However, Philip restored the man's hope by giving witness to the Good News. His words of passion for God were instantly rewarded.

Pastor Graham and his wife Mairi (who as a minister-in-training shared the message with us) highlighted again the changing face of The Church since lockdown. Unable to meet in communal spaces, with places of prayer and worship closed since March, the message of salvation in

Christ has subsequently moved to the 'fringes'. Physically, we may have been 'off-line' but in its place God's online presence has been manifolded. Mairi noted how in times when the church, in this country and elsewhere, has needed to move to the margins of society, great revival has occurred. The church in China, a case in point, where 60 million Christians now live, despite open persecution and social prejudice.

Are we now in a time of faith marginalisation in the UK? If so, is this conversely the exact right time to spread the Word with conviction and passion? Mairi spoke about her 'audacious hope' in this time of pandemic and beyond. Even as we are eased out of our physical inertia back into a world of face to face inter-connections, it is important the gains we have seen whilst communicating on the fringes are not lost. The thousands, if not millions of people sitting in their chariots seeking a better Truth are depending on it.

7th July: *Sticky Situation*

One of my favourite TV shows of all time is the Blackadder series with Rowan Atkinson in the title role; a frustrated character surrounded by a motley collection of hapless dimwits. The show is known for its great one-liners, usually uttered by Blackadder himself. On one occasion in the final series, *Blackadder Goes Forth* set in the Great War, Captain Blackadder finds himself as usual in a perilous crises and utters in despair, 'We're in the stickiest situation since Sticky the Stick Insect got stuck on a sticky bun.' It is a moment of comedy genius and these words spring to mind every time I witness (or am more directly party to) the unravelling of a series of events that can only end in tears.

You know the moments I mean, surely? The time when you realise you have overslept on the train home and missed your stop by thirty miles. You have no money, and it was the last train to run either way on the same route. No? How about, when the car runs out of petrol in the middle of bear country, the days when mobile phones had not yet been invented? No? Or, you walk into the wrong pub in Eastern Europe and wait for the friend who is not going to appear; the drunk locals get twitchy and realise you are a 'rich tourist from the UK'? *No*? Well, you have not lived friends!

Anyway, here is a classic example straight from the heart of the Surrey commuter belt which has left locals totally dumfounded. On the 3rd July Surrey County Council began preparing to trial a new cycle lane coupled with a widening of pavements along Reigate High Street. This was part of a match-funding Government Scheme aimed at increasing access for cyclists riding through town centres; and the widening of pedestrian routes to support social distancing. Existing loading bays were suspended to increase pedestrian space and the cycle lane construction would reduce the one-way traffic flow from two lanes to one. This would link up the cycle path at the end of the town centre, with a 20 mph suggested speed limit. On the face of it, a neat plan with a touch of *green-is-good* to it.

However, just three days later the scheme has been scraped, the new signage and bollards removed, and the traffic flow has reverted back to two lanes. In the days in between, the only good thing from this situation was that nobody got hurt! For its size, Reigate High Street must be one of the busiest in England, situated on the A25 between the commuter run of Crawley and Dorking. Normally two lanes strain to take the traffic load during peak times, and the shops rely on the loading zones for deliveries. One end of the street is particularly tight for lorries to squeeze round, and there is parking along one side so cars have to quickly make for any empty space, often causing those behind to swerve into the other lane. Take one of the two traffic lanes away and you start to get the picture. *Mayhem*

The final straw came when an ambulance could not make its way through the one line of traffic - with nowhere to go, the cars just sat there marooned like whales on a beach. Furthermore, the A25 is also a main artery between several towns and the nearby East Surrey Hospital. Whoever came up with this scheme (I will omit names here to protect further embarrassment), *what were they thinking?* I am only writing this piece in the blog today, because, as one says...*you just cannot make it up!*

Situations like this tend to come down to one thing. *Consultation.* Or in this case, a seemingly lack of it. The list of those who knew nothing about the changes to the High Street before it happened includes the Reigate Business Guild, the local Residents' Associations, and regional NHS stakeholders. Consulting those who have a vested interest before jumping in with two feet would have saved much angst. It seems the Council received this government grant and got a bit over-excited. The moral of the tale is before, what Blackadder's little side-kick Baldrick would call '*a cunning plan*' is hatched, it is best to prepare the groundwork first.

Thankfully, God has both a plan for the whole world and a plan for each of our lives. In challenging times our faith in these plans may be tested, and we may even openly question God's reasons and intentions as we struggle to comprehend the brokenness around us. Yet, the Bible makes it abundantly clear. God's planning for His own creation is full proof. How do we know this? The life, death and resurrection of Jesus Christ provides the perfect blueprint from which The Father's purposes are to ultimately be fulfilled. Through Christ, salvation is guaranteed, and His Glory will one-day be restored on Earth as it is in Heaven. That is just more Good News for us all. There are no sticky buns in heaven.

'For I know the plans I have for you,' declares the Lord, 'plans to prosper you and not to harm you, plans to give you hope and a future.'

Jeremiah 29 v11

9th July: *The Sound of Music*

Sorry to disappoint any fans of Julie Andrews, but I am not referring here to the legendary musical. I was actually in the college building all day today, this time to help assess the practical element of a teacher training course. Unlike my brief visit into work last week, I was mentally ready for the challenge of the one-way system and the eerie quietness of a campus, which should have been filled with the bustle of students and staff.

In one of the short teaching sessions I observed, the deliverer chose to share his specialist subject area, *song writing*. Having dabbled with this creative artform myself since my teens, I was as intrigued as the audience - made up of other adult trainees. We were asked to consider the different techniques used by artists when writing a contemporary pop song. So by analysing the words and music of *Before You Go* by Lewis Capaldi, we began to pick out the way the rhythm, the arrangement and the words merged together to create an emotional response in the listener. In essence we were delving into the song's heart and soul.

Music is often regarded as the heartbeat of a nation's culture, and as such often mirrors the socio-economic landscape of the day. Logically, you would think in times of hardship and even fear, song writing would reflect this with a stream of darkened melodies, slow dragging backbeats and anti-establishment lyrics. Surely in the middle of a global pandemic the contemporary music charts should be full of the moody blues? Yet, the evidence suggests the opposite. For in 2020, research shows an increase in the tempo of songs being released both sides of the Atlantic, with a shift towards catchy pop melodies and a greater positivity in the lyric. Some of the music was of course written pre-pandemic, but there is sufficient evidence to suggest there has been 'an important psychological change' (Charlie Harding, Switched On Pop).

In fact, there have been previous links between downcast living and upbeat music, notably during the Great Depression and World War Two. Harding refers to the wave of escapism music which seeks to 'give us permission to access joy, even when the world is burning'. Music can be written to combine a sense of pride and purpose in oneself with a *let's blow off steam and go out dancing vibe*. Several artists including Lady Gaga and Raye have announced their intention to create more uplifting sounds which take us from current despair to an ideal future. Even when the lyrics suggest struggle and frustration, the overall impact is one of hope for a better tomorrow. Raye sums up the conflicting emotions in writing songs during lockdown.

'It's a real battle between do I address how I feel and what's going on, or do I just create something that feels the opposite? But I think if we were to be sitting on Zoom writing ballads, we'd just feel depressed, so it makes sense to channel this upbeat 80s vibe.'

As a product of the 80s who got his teenage kicks out of high energy dance music from Kylie and Wham, I welcome the shift. No smirking please. I also enjoyed the melancholier undertones of The Smiths, The Cure, Tears for Fears and my favourite band of all, the wonderfully eclectic Talk Talk. Credibility restored.

If music is indeed the *food of love,* this pandemic has starved many, leaving a sense of emptiness, and the younger generation in particular with quite an appetite. Local live music concerts, larger events such as The Isle of Wight Festival and Glastonbury, and open-air concerts in the park, have been taken away from us at a time when we needed them the most. So, it was very welcome news yesterday when Oliver Dowden, Secretary of State for Digital, Culture, Media and Sport (should be the best job in the world really?) announced the reopening of outdoor concert venues and theatres. Measures for safe performing are still being thrashed out but include how singers should position themselves side-to-side or back-to-back, and musicians observing safe social distancing.

This statement comes hot on the heels of a £1.57 billion bailout for the wider arts industry. As well as funding to bring back live music venues, this rescue package will go towards the supporting of museums, galleries, theatres, and heritage sites. With so many actors, musicians and curators staring unemployment in the face as the furlough scheme fades out, the government may have averted a crisis at the very heart of our cultural heritage. The hope now is singing can soon be introduced back into indoor venues such as concert halls and places of worship. Then, for those of us who enjoy singing as a vital part of faith, fellowship and praise, we can let loose the vocal cords once more. The hills of England's green and pleasant land may then again come alive with the sound of music.

Out of interest the hymn *Jerusalem*, possibly the number one choice of pews up and down the country, was originally written as a poem by William Blake in 1804. The lyrics were added to music written by Hubert Parry in 1916 during the gloom of WWI when an uplifting new English hymn was needed. Stirring stuff indeed!

>Bring me my bow of burning gold!
>Bring me my arrows of desire!
>Bring me my spear! O clouds, unfold!
>Bring me my chariot of fire!
>I will not cease from mental fight,
>Nor shall my sword sleep in my hand,
>Till we have built Jerusalem
>In England's green and pleasant land.

11th July: *Identity*

Last night I introduced Diana to one of my favourite films of the 1980s, *Out of Africa*. I had not watched it myself for many years, but if like my wife you appreciate a good old romantic weepy then this is right up there. The East African landscape is breath-taking, and Meryl Streep and Robert Redford prowl around each other like mating lions. Yet this is a story, based on the written memoirs of Streep's character Karen Blixen, about individual identity in a time of great social change in the early part of the C20th.

Blixen, financially wealthy but socially outcast in her native Denmark, moves to Kenya to find a new sense of purpose. She immediately marries a Baron, gaining a title and status. He in turn, broke and of ill-repute, gains her endowment and a new zeal for life. The marriage soon unravels with Baron Blor Blixen disinterested in the coffee plantation his wife's money has bought, preferring to blend into the colonial culture of poaching. In the long periods of absence, the lonely Baroness falls for the free-spirited hunter and guide Denys Finch Hatton. It is then the notion of personal identity comes to the fore.

This entangled triangle pulls each of the three protagonists into an ever-complex circle of self-fulfilment and self-doubt. Baron Blor Blixen seeks public recognition with his fellow masochistic big game hunters, trying to live up to the weight of expectation his title brings. Joining the rag tag army of Western European colonials to fight a common foe, also gives him the credence he lost in his native Denmark. In choosing this path he loses the love of his wife, who came to Africa to find a different identity; fulfilment through a sense of destiny, and to fall in love with someone who will share that dream. It is not surprising therefore that Karen's empty void is filled by a man who offers her what she seeks. Yet Denys Finch Hatton is bound not to this human ideal, but to the ideal of freedom itself. This is epitomised in his desire to learn to fly, to be totally unabandoned and accountable to no-one, not even to the desirable Baroness. When Karen questions his lack of commitment, Denys' response strikes at the heart of the self-identity theme:

I'm with you because I choose to be with you. I don't want to live someone else's idea of how to live. Don't ask me to do that. I don't want to find out one day that I'm at the end of someone else's life.

Yet by the end of the film there is a disclosure from each character which cuts through the mask of the identity they had worn so adamantly throughout. Baron Blor Blixen has tired of running from responsibility and marries again (for money of course) but regrets the years lost taking Karen for granted. Denys also realises freedom and commitment are not mutually exclusive and confesses to Karen how much he is going to miss her as she leaves Africa for the last time.

Denys: You've ruined it for me, you know.
Karen: Ruined what?
Denys: Being alone.

As for Karen Blixen herself, the romantic dream of Africa has gone. The coffee plantation has been devastated by fire, and with Denys revealing his feelings too late, she moves back to Denmark, broke in every sense of the word. In the last years of her life, Karen finds her identity once more, but not in a romantic escapist dream, but in the arms of her Danish family back in the roots of her native home.

For so many of us living in our relative comfort, the notion of self-identity has become a central part of our belief and value systems. For young people in particular, the pressure to *fit in* and find an identify that defines their own personal value system is more complex than ever. Arguably, it is one of the root causes of the increase in anxiousness and poor mental health in modern society. The coronavirus pandemic has added to this stress, by disrupting the natural patterns of life, and putting plans, dreams and hopes either on hold, or leaving them in tatters. Covid-19 has stripped away the security of health, work, family and even friends. It has turned the world of millions upside down, and in doing so left self-identity hiding in the shadows.

As the wearing of masks becomes more commonplace, there is a physical imagery here too, with our natural self-hidden from others.

Masks signify secrecy and deception: think Venice masquerades and Batman. Our challenge as we emerge out of lockdown is to remain true to ourselves and not hide behind a mask. As Christians we must not lose sight of where our true identity lies. Human frailties and inherent sinful nature will lead us to rely on money, wealth, status, sexuality, career, earthly passions and *living the dream* as the foundation of our identity. However, these things are fragile compared to the assuredness of God's Love for us. The Bible tells us to rely on the 'rock of our salvation', and the testimony of millions worldwide confirm this to be the case. In Christ, our *identity* is set for eternity, and that is something worth treasuring now.

For he chose us in him before the creation of the world to be holy and blameless in his sight. In love he predestined us for adoption to sonship through Jesus Christ, in accordance with his pleasure and will Ephesians 4 v5

12th July: *Shaken and ...Stirred*

How would you react if an angel woke you up from a deep sleep one night and told you to get dressed and follow him? Well that is just what happened to the disciple Peter, the leader of the early church in Jerusalem. Continuing the Sunday morning series from the Book of Acts, Pastor Graham led the online congregation through the story of Peter's miraculous escape from prison. Arrested on the authority of the Jewish king Herod, Peter is left naked and chained, guarded by four squads of four soldiers. Acts 12 4:17 reads...

After arresting him, he put him in prison, handing him over to be guarded by four squads of four soldiers each. Herod intended to bring him out for public trial after the Passover.

So Peter was kept in prison, but the church was earnestly praying to God for him.

When we are facing troubled times, how earnestly do we pray?

The night before Herod was to bring him to trial, Peter was sleeping between two soldiers, bound with two chains, and sentries stood guard at the entrance.

Who do we turn to when there seems no escape from fear and darkness?

Suddenly an angel of the Lord appeared, and a light shone in the cell. He struck Peter on the side and woke him up. "Quick, get up!" he said, and the chains fell off Peter's wrists.

Then the angel said to him, "Put on your clothes and sandals." And Peter did so. "Wrap your cloak around you and follow me," the angel told him.

However irrational God's response may feel, how ready are we to follow Him when He answers our prayers?

Peter followed him out of the prison, but he had no idea that what the angel was doing was really happening; he thought he was seeing a vision.

They passed the first and second guards and came to the iron gate leading to the city. It opened for them by itself, and they went through it. When they had walked the length of one street, suddenly the angel left him.

Are we obedient in our journey of faith, even when we cannot see the way ahead?

Then Peter came to himself and said, "Now I know without a doubt that the Lord has sent his angel and rescued me from Herod's clutches and from everything the Jewish people were hoping would happen."

When this had dawned on him, he went to the house of Mary the mother of John, also called Mark, where many people had gathered and were praying.

When there is no doubt who is in control, how do we then react?

Peter knocked at the outer entrance, and a servant named Rhoda came to answer the door.

When she recognized Peter's voice, she was so overjoyed she ran back without opening it and exclaimed, "Peter is at the door!"

"You're out of your mind," they told her. When she kept insisting that it was so, they said, "It must be his angel."

But Peter kept on knocking, and when they opened the door and saw him, they were astonished.

When God reveals Himself in our lives, do we still doubt His presence?

Peter motioned with his hand for them to be quiet and described how the Lord had brought him out of prison. "Tell James and the other brothers and sisters about this," he said, and then he left for another place.

How passionate are we to tell others how God has transformed our lives?

When God awakes us from our slumbers, He often shakes us to the core. The angel did not tap Peter on the shoulder and whisper in his ear, but struck the disciple firmly on his side, awaking him with a start. That is the easy part! It is how we react that matters; do we stir ourselves to action or pretend it is all a dream? Eventually Peter came to his full senses and realised who was in charge. This story of God's power to deliver us from the greatest of dangers is also a clear message that prayer is part of the deal. As a church, prayer has to be at the centre of our mission to transform not only ourselves, but our friends and families, and the wider community around us.

14th July: *Painting by Numbers*

There are a few things I wish I was much better at. This includes a long list of 'ings' such as swimming, singing, plumbing, cooking and gardening. However, the one talent which really fills me with envy is drawing/painting. Whether it was marvelling at my school friends who did A level Art or being inspired by the Masters such as Van Gogh and Monet. I just wish I could put pencil or brush to paper and create an image that actually looked like the original subject. Since the age of five, I have dabbled with crayons, Etch-A-Sketch, Spirograph, and watercolours, but the best artwork I have managed was a selection of Marvel characters when in my mid-teens. Ok, The Incredible Hulk looked more like The Jolly Green Giant, and Iron Man resembled Robbie the Robot - but hey, I gave it a go. As a come-lately *man of words* trying to convey ideas as best he can using the English language as a guide, I ooze with jealousy when a gifted artist can paint a thousand words, the finished picture to be interpreted in a many ways. It is a powerful medium.

Sarah is now back in Reading and looking forward to making her new student house feel like home. Her bedroom back here now looks as clean and tidy as it did pre-lockdown, and her brother took little time moving the drum kit back upstairs where it now sits between Sarah's chest of drawers and the bed once more. In the tidy up process, I came across a few of Sarah's pieces of artwork she did as part of her AS Level two years ago. One of them is a line drawing of her best friend Izzy, with gentle pastel colours bringing out the warmth in her face. Coming out of the right-hand side of Izzy's head, Sarah painted two clock faces showing two different times. I am not sure about the deep meaning behind the picture, but it certainly leaves an impression. Such talent, and for Sarah art was really just a hobby, which for those of us drawing poorly imagined superheroes, is a bit annoying.

So talking of gifted artists, the enigma that is Banksy has been up to mischief again. This time, dressed as a cleaner on the London

Underground, Banksy went to work on the inside of a tube train carriage. A released video clip, to prove it was the elusive Bristol based street artist in action, showed how he used a stencil to paint several rats, with one rat using a surgical mask as a parachute! Another rodent is then painted holding a bottle of hand sanitiser, followed by the word 'Banksy' sprayed at the end of the carriage in recognisable street art style. A final message, as if needed, accompanied the video clip, a caption saying: '*If you don't mask - you don't get*'. A reference to the announcement by Boris Johnson just 24 hours earlier stating everyone will have to wear face coverings in shops from 24 July.

Sadly, this latest masterpiece had a short lifespan. Unaware of the significance of the graffiti artwork, 'real' Transport for London (TfL) cleaning staff scrubbed off the images and signature before the video had been seen by senior managers. This was even more wasteful given Banksy's clear message that wearing masks was encouraged whilst travelling by tube. A TfL spokesperson was quick to provide a piece of public relations damage limitation.

'In this particular case, the work was removed some days ago due to our strict anti-graffiti policy. We'd like to offer Banksy the chance to do a new version of this message for our customers in a suitable location'

A noble offer indeed, but Banksy is a law unto himself, and he may not oblige repeating this scenario. The whole saga is doubly tragic, if the expert opinion of art guru Joey Syer is on the money. Syer is the co-founder of a firm which has specialised in buying and selling Banksy's work all around the world to the rich and powerful.

'Had TfL management known and had the opportunity to remove and protect the installation, we estimate it's value as a complete package to be in the region of £7.7 million'.

Lovely! Just to let you all know, I have a brilliant picture in my possession from a little-known artist now living in the bohemian part of Reading. I will start the bidding at £25,000..........

15th July: *Praise Sandwich*

When you read many of David's Psalms, they often begin with Praise for God and end in the same way,', explained Chris after we read Psalm 7 together as an online Church Growth Group. *'A bit like a praise sandwich!'* I interjected with a Zoom smirk on my face. Several blank faces peered back at me as though I had spoken in Urdu. *'It's a phrase we use in teaching'*, Diana voiced, coming to my rescue. *'Oh?'*, said Jan who wanted like the others a bit more of an explanation. I felt a sudden duty to oblige.

'When we give written feedback to our students the praise sandwich is often used. You start with positive feedback, praising the student for something they have done well, followed by your points of constructive criticism, and then end with another more positive comment.' I was now in full flow. *'So an example could be, thank you for nearly submitting this work on time....you shouldn't have bothered, it was horrendous...keep going though as there's still a slim chance you will pass this course.'* Too much satire. They thought I was being serious.

Anyway, Chris brought the group back on track with real words of wisdom. *'Er, thank you Paul, let's all see how King David acknowledges God as His shelter and protector in times of trouble in these opening verses.'*

> Lord my God, I take refuge in you;
>   save and deliver me from all who pursue me,
> or they will tear me apart like a lion
>   and rip me to pieces with no one to rescue me.

The middle part of the Psalm certainly shifts the mood to a much darker tone. David pleads with God to send His wrath on the King's enemies, who showed little respect for God and King.

Whoever is pregnant with evil
conceives trouble and gives birth to disillusionment.
Whoever digs a hole and scoops it out
falls into the pit they have made.
The trouble they cause recoils on them;
their violence comes down on their own heads.

Well that is telling them Dave! No holds barred- a bit of constructive criticism there for sure. Let us not forget the more positive praise ending to acknowledge who is in charge:

I will give thanks to the Lord because of his righteousness;
I will sing the praises of the name of the Lord Most High.

This feedback technique is not just the domain of teachers and Old Testament Kings. The government briefings which took place daily in the first twelve weeks of lockdown provided a classic example of the praise sandwich in action. The minister on call would start with some positive messages about how well the government was dealing with the pandemic, often praising the NHS for their contribution to this success. Then would come the barrage of constructive criticism through the media question and answer section, and the briefing would finish back with the minister reminding everyone how together we would beat Covid-19, and that supremo Boris is totally on top of things.

Talking of the prime minister and the management of 'feedback' Boris Johnson has, under some pressure, agreed to an independent inquiry. Not now, but in the future, he declares. This inquiry will focus on how the UK Government has handled the pandemic, and whether any lessons can be learned. Criticism of the government response has come from many quarters and focuses on the number of deaths (now at over 45,000) in the UK compared to other countries like Germany and France. One group, Covid-19 Bereaved Families for Justice says the PM has refused to meet them to discuss their concerns and are worried any inquiry will not come soon enough.

This has got me thinking. How would we feel if there was an 'independent inquiry' at the end of our lives? I would hope at least the inquisitor would use the praise sandwich method to soften the blow a bit. Here are a few positive highlights first, followed by a less than impressive middle section of 'constructive criticism', and rounded off with a *'you tried hard, gave it a go...and thank you for turning up'*. Fortunately for us, God's grace has intervened. Through acknowledging the sacrifice of Jesus, we can come to our own independent inquiry in confidence that the middle section has been wiped clean. Unlike King David, who relied solely on his own faithful words of petition to plead with God, we now have the assurance that Christ has already petitioned with the Father on our behalf.

16th July: *Cyber Wars*

The coronavirus pandemic has focused the human mind on many things. One of the socio-cultural shifts in the UK since lockdown has been the way online technologies have taken a more prominent place in our everyday lives. Millions have been working from home, often with little or no detrimental impact on business activities, and thousands of school pupils and college students have engaged in remote learning in a way not experienced before. This has meant a rapid upskilling of digital skills and investment in infrastructure, so inter-connectivity between individuals and companies is efficient and reliable. Social media platforms have come to the fore as tools for the advancement of information (my journey into the world of Twitter would have been highly unlikely pre-Covid), and Microsoft and Google have enjoyed a further rise towards world domination.

Against this backdrop something sinister is afoot. This week the UK government has banned the Chinese tech giant Huawei from future 5G networks following months of concern that their equipment could be used to spy on data and citizens. In a transatlantic show of unity, the US administration have also announced the same strategy which has accelerated trade tensions between themselves and China. The Chinese have already warned the UK retaliation will be forthcoming. This situation, coming on the back of accusations towards China about the origins of Covid-19, and national criticism of the imposition of Chinese law on the former UK territory Hong Kong, will further exacerbate the strains between East and West.

As if that is not worrying enough, the UK, US and Canadian security services are accusing Russian cyber hackers of targeting organisations trying to develop a coronavirus vaccine. The UK's National Cyber Security Centre says the hackers 'almost certainly' operated as 'part of Russian intelligence services'. Today, the Russian authorities have vehemently denied any knowledge of the hacking. It is all very James Bond.

As much as I like a good conspiracy theory - the Loch Ness monster exists, aliens built Stonehenge, Elvis still lives etc - this cyber stuff is all now quite concerning. Accusation and counter-accusation is a norm between countries with different ideologies but the use of computer technology is an integral part of our daily routines. My son for instance has just assembled his own desk top computer, sourcing the parts from a variety of online companies. This *'well done Daniel on your GCSE grades-early birthday-very early Christmas* present' now sits in his bedroom, a cross between a small spaceship and the Blackpool illuminations. For a parent, it is a slight concern that my son has the skills and means to launch his own cyber-attack on an unsuspecting country or multinational company. There is now a million times more technology in my son's bedroom than NASA had available when putting a man on the Moon in 1969.

Of course, the moon-landing did not actually happen. I have read enough online material to know that without a doubt this event was a film studio mock-up just to peeve the Russians. Oh, and did you know there is a Yeti living in a Chinese zoo called Brian?

17th July: *Longevity*

Today, after waiting for over four months Diana and myself finally got the thing that was starting to grind us both down. A professional haircut! Hallelujah, and praise the Lord for our two lovely ladies who are now back snipping and colouring away in their small but perfectly formed salon in neighbouring Bletchingly. One of my favourite scenes in the film version of Educating Rita, is where an elderly client, pointing to a magazine picture, asks hairdresser Rita to transform her wiry grey mop into the flowing locks of Princess Diana. In similar fashion, every time we are about to visit our hairdressers, my princess Diana is surfing the internet trying to find the ultimate transformation. It is usually a toss-up between a 'Danni Minogue' and a 'Halle Berry', which all seems pretty good in my books. However, there is an obvious flaw to this exercise, but I can't quite put my finger on it!

This time with extra months of growth to play with, Diana brought up pictures of Beyonce onto our laptop. I pointed out there were fashion hairstyles for the more *mature look* to be found on other websites. Diana replied that I looked like cousin 'Itt' from the Adams Family, and if I did not want her to use gardening shears to 'reduce me to a hedge cutting' then I should keep my views to myself. Not wanting to look like a scalped shrubbery, I kept stum until we reached the promised land of Bletchingly. The outcome was very pleasing indeed. *Beyonce* and I returned home feeling somewhat liberated as if the weight of the world had lifted from our shoulders. Diana was back to her dark sultry best and I was happy that my thin lifeless Anglo-Saxon mop looked once more at home on my small white crown.

That brings me to the real highlight of the day. In fact, it could be the highlight of the whole lockdown period! For at Windsor Castle this afternoon Captain Tom Moore received a knighthood from the Queen as a result of his raising £32.7 million for NHS charities. It was a touching sight, the 94-year-old monarch brandishing a sword across the shoulders of the 100-year-old army veteran. So many years, so many memories between them, both having seen incredible change in their lifetimes since the early part of the 20th Century. Yet, for most of the British public, all we have known is Elizabeth as our Queen. During her 67 year reign she has been served by fourteen prime ministers, seen the rise and fall of the Berlin Wall, ruled during several military campaigns and the Cold War in Europe, and seen the emergence of the new digital age. She has also seen enormous change in the Royal Family itself, as protocols and expectations have needed to adapt to the ways of the modern World.

Through all this change, Elizabeth has been a fixed entity, standing like a rock in the middle of a turbulent sea. She has stood firm, carrying out her duties with dignity and pride, and in return even the most ardent republicans I suspect have respected her great resilience. Yet if you asked the Queen where her strength of character and resolve comes from, she would not hesitate in declaring the importance of her Christian faith. In her Christmas speech to the nation in 2000 the Queen made it very clear what has sustained her all these years;

'For me the teachings of Christ and my own personal accountability before God provide a framework in which I try to lead my life. I, like so many of you, have drawn great comfort in difficult times from Christ's words and example.'

For many of us, the Queen serves as a great inspiration. She has been the epitome of longevity. Yet, her personal testimony of faith reminds us who we should ultimately place of trust in. The sands of time will catch up with all of us, and even our greatest living monarch will pass away one day.

Our very humanity makes us as fragile as the hairs on our heads. Today the coronavirus pandemic blows a seemingly uncontrollable wind of fear over all nations. In this sense, it could be argued, nothing lasts forever. Nothing that is except for the God who we believe is the Creator and ruler of all things. His reign lasts forever, and His character does not change. We also see this in the character of Jesus Christ who sits at His Father's right hand. If we ever fear the changing patterns of life, let us focus on the one who *'is the same yesterday, today and forevermore'* Hebrews 13 v8

18th July: *Prayer for the World*

The latest statistics from around the world continue to make grim reading. I feel I have written that line too many times since the middle of March. In the UK we are inching out of lockdown, as though the government is feeling its way in the dark, hoping things will turn out right. Working towards economic recovery now seems to be the pacemaker in the race back to normality, with the numbers of cases and deaths back to pre-lockdown levels. Isolated but still significant outbreaks on the 'mainland' are reported but no longer make the headlines on the evening news. Step by step, Europe edges its way out of lockdown. Back on the path, but not out of the woods.

However, the Americas, Africa and Asia have now all been defined as Covid hotspots. That is three massive hotspots! The global number of infections now stands at 14.3 million (John Hopkins University). Today, the number of cases in the last 24 hours rose by a record 260,000. Brazil has over two million reported cases. Cases in India are doubling every 20 days. According to the World Health Organisation, more than 600,000 people have died with the coronavirus, nearly a quarter of this total in the USA. Donald Trump is threatening to send US Federal troops into states where the virus is surging. It is the latest desperate intervention from a president who has struggled to hold a tight grip on his nation's response to the pandemic.

This is not just my inference. Dan is constructing a family tree using an online ancestry app and is doing really well to locate various distant aunties and uncles on Diana's side. It has led him to family based in San Francisco, first and second generation Indian Americans originating from Karachi and Mangalore. *What stories they shared!* Speaking on Whatsapp, they told us about their experiences of settling into a new life in California. The best tales of the unexpected however, came from 93-year-old Auntie Theresa who despite ill health was as bright as a button, recalling passages from India in great detail. Her sense of time and place undiminished by her years, articulating memories as though they were yesterday. We all agreed she was more with it than most. Just this morning I found myself upstairs staring into space unable to fathom out why I had made the journey from the lounge in the first place. Not my first senior moment.

Dan was delighted to find out more information about his Indian grandparents (Diana's late parents), how they eloped from Goa to London in the 1950s on a steamboat, and the reaction of family back in India. One day I would love to write this story with its colours of love, passion, hardship and struggle. For now, I return to my original point. Having listened to various relatives in several parts of North America, they had one thing in common: a dislike for their president. Even those who once gave him the benefit of the doubt have lost patience. 'Buffoon' was the kindest descriptive word I can write here. The consensus was clear. There would be another President of the United States of America in the Whitehouse as a result of the November election.

As we enter the peak Summer holiday period in a lockdown-easing Europe, the urge to flee to sunny shores and let the hair down at home and abroad will be at the forefront of many minds. For others it will be thoughts of when their next pay check will arrive. *If at all*. A post-Covid era of critical reflection has started, and one discussion focus has been the role of lessor paid manual jobs in the UK. Another is the high fatality rate in England and Wales compared to the relative size of population. The accusations and counter-accusations are beginning to surface with greater intensity, and after the way Brexit has divided the country for nearly four years, further lines of division could further fracture our fragile land.

It seems fitting for the blog today to choose a prayer for these times from a lady in Seattle. Cameron Wiggins Bellm released this into the public domain via the internet in March. It has proved to be a blessing to many individuals and churches since and reminds those of us who live in relative comfort about those who do not.

May we who are merely inconvenienced
Remember those whose lives are at stake.
May we who have no risk factors
Remember those most vulnerable.
May we who have the luxury of working from home
Remember those who must choose between preserving their health or making their rent.
May we who have the flexibility to care for our children when their schools close
Remember those who have no options.
May we who have to cancel our trips
Remember those that have no safe place to go.
May we who are losing our margin money in the tumult of the economic market
Remember those who have no margin at all.
May we who settle in for a quarantine at home
Remember those who have no home.
As fear grips our country,
let us choose love.
During this time when we cannot physically wrap our arms around each other,
Let us yet find ways to be the loving embrace of God to our neighbours.
Amen.

19th July: *On the Frontline*

As Christians, the greatest challenge we often face is how to best share our faith in secular contexts, away from the cosiness that comes from being with like-minded friends, family, and the wider church fellowship. Pastor Graham refers to this as our frontline, where the spiritual battleground is often far more significant than our more comfortable encounters in less threatening settings. The secular context Graham argues, be it at work, in the playground, in the pub, in the shopping centre, represents the frontline where God wants us to be sharing our faith, helping those who often need practical and emotional support. Our secular roles in society, notably the 'job' which defines us the most, becomes a key part of the frontline for Jesus.

The coronavirus pandemic has created an enlightened change in attitude towards those job roles which have traditionally been undervalued. Our perspective of careers that traditionally are characterised by servitude and the mundane have during lockdown become important cogs in the fight against the collective invisible enemy. In response, we clapped the NHS and key workers every Thursday on our doorsteps for ten weeks. We have also been indebted to cleaners, health workers, bus drivers, delivery drivers, refuse workers, hospital porters and those employed in community care services. A report out this week shows how the pandemic is changing the world of work. In general terms, the trend of working from home is going to lead to a huge shift in the nations' working patterns, especially for *white collar commuters*. Already in suburban Surrey, the demand for property has escalated in July as Londoners see the attraction of moving to relatively affordable family homes. One reason cited by local estate agents is the growth of homeworking as a new viable option. The other reason I hear is the need for a large garden! The urban English are going *green*. Lockdown has certainly re-ordered and re-prioritised our lifestyle values.

However, this report on changing employment trends from *CV-Library* is not good news for school and college leavers. The number of job vacancies in the UK fell by over 60% in the second business quarter of

2020. For those jobs being advertised, the application-to-job ratio has gone sky high. Recently we heard about a £9 per hour bar job in South London for which there were 484 applicants! Some companies though are flourishing, expanding their workforce to meet the needs of the new normal. These include IT and digital technology businesses, warehouse pickers and delivery drivers, supermarkets and food retail, lorry drivers, and domestic cleaners. Delivery giant Hermes for instance says it will create 10,500 jobs in the UK after seeing a surge in demand for online shopping during lockdown. On the flipside we have seen significant job losses in high street shops, non-food retail, pubs and restaurants, the events industry and in aviation. IAG, the parent company of British Airways recently warned it could take several years for air travel to return to 2019 levels.

Yesterday, the government has also recognised the contribution of 900,000 public sector workers with an above-inflation pay rise for teachers, NHS dentists, the police, prison officers, and armed forces personnel. Calls for those in social care to also receive a 'coronavirus reward' have gone unheeded, and accusations that ministers are misleading workers with many hidden caveats in this pay award demonstrates the risk to further social division.

Some of us are blessed to have relative security in our current frontline. Although working in a different way, Diana and myself will basically be doing what we were doing in March, in the same buildings, with the same colleagues around us. The *psychology* of these frontlines may be where the challenges and the opportunities arise. It will not just be the mental health and well-being of students put to the test when schools and colleges fully reconvene, for staff too will take time to re-adjust. There have been times, for instance, when the removal of a natural boundary between home and work has knocked me out of my stride. *Only* communicating on screen for months has numbed the senses, and it has been a reminder that there is no real substitute for face to face interaction.

Wherever our frontline may be, and however humble our daily tasks may feel, we must take heart in the knowledge we are exactly where God wants us....today. In our *today* we can take confidence in knowing who we are serving, and what the ultimate rewards will be.

Whatever you do, work at it with all your heart, as working for the Lord, not for human masters, since you know that you will receive an inheritance from the Lord as a reward. It is the Lord Christ you are serving.
Colossians 3 v23-24

20th July: *Pecking Order*

Now *that is* a good feeling. I awake today knowing the work laptop does not have to be turned on at 8.45 a.m. I have been doing this for months, just in case I am sent that all important email to which if I do not reply straight away could mean the end of civilisation as we know it. *Hallelujah*, I have a three week holiday break for the Summer, and so it is time to unplug that work lap top, hide the work phone in my sock draw, and file the work diary under the floorboards. Basically, I am going *off grid*, just like Jason Bourne or Ethan Hunt. But is this attempt at cutting oneself off from the world of work *mission impossible?*

Diana doubts whether I can do this considering I have been 'on call' from home for eighteen weeks. As noted previously the danger of homeworking is the lack of tangible boundaries, and many colleagues have found it difficult to switch between work and non-work mode. Those of us new to this change in working culture have discovered through lockdown a phenomenon I call 'online guilt complex'. If we miss an email, or even worse, the sudden request for a screen meeting, then we feel guilty about it. We also start thinking to ourselves, *'what if the boss feels I am not working as hard as I should?'* or *'I don't want anyone thinking I am not coping at home!'*. This complex over time inevitably leads to increases in anxiety and stress.

I *have* enjoyed some of the elements of home-working, like the on-tap coffee machine, the freedom to take a ten minute time-out away from the lap-top, or when Mo 'helps' me with work by walking across my keyboard at the most inopportune time. On the negative side, eye-strain, the lack of personal communication, and the aforementioned guilt-creep has not been such fun.

Three weeks to fill then... mostly at home, which this year is not going to be much of a scenery change. We decided going abroad on a late deal was not for us, and besides this Summer we have a furry pup to look after. Fortunately, bearing this in mind we booked a week away for the three of us pre-Covid and we are subsequently heading for the English

South Coast next week. Of course, now we have Jess, the conversation around holiday options changes completely. Her needs come first, whether that is taking her with us, or leaving her behind with others. To be honest Dan and Daniel have trouble looking after themselves most days, and my son is spending a week with his birth mother anyway. Dan therefore will house sit and is dreading looking after Mo and his weird toilet habits. *We are only an hour away Dan, so if you need us in an emergency etc. etc...However, you know where the bathroom cleaner is!*

I am assuming every family has a priority pecking order. Don't they?

Last year the *pecking order* in our family home was far more complicated! You know about poor old Lottie (natural causes). We also lost Mo's sister called Beth (kidney failure) and a lovely fifteen-year-old Labrador called Keedra (natural causes). If I had written this blog in 2019 it would have been called *My Animals and Other Family*, such was the dominance of the pets on our lives. I could really generalise here, by saying the 'man in your average nuclear household' is usually at the back of the family pecking order. But I won't say this, as I do not like to be controversial. It is just often the natural order of things that children come at the top, the homemaker comes a tight second, the family pets take the bronze, and the breakfast guru/light entertainer/super-uber/wasp killer figure trundles in a distant last. I am sure this is different in Eastern cultures, but in Surrey suburbia it seems like the norm, and I have no problem with it at all.

I am in the lounge on the phone, protecting my cup of tea from Jess, when a cry echoes around the house. *'Paul, come and see this, upstairs...quick. You are not going to believe this!'* I grunted in fluent caveman. *'No quickly, you will miss this. Bring the binoculars from the study.'* I grabbed the 'bins' as we say in bird twitching speak, and climbed the stairs wondering if Diana was about to show me a squirrel dancing on the clothesline, or a pair of mating pigeons.

Arriving in our bedroom, the roof Velux window was wide open, and Diana was peering out at the back garden. It was not an acrobatic squirrel, nor a pair of romantic pigeons. It was something quite extraordinary...and very rare. On the lawn pecking away was a Green Woodpecker, an infrequent visitor to the neighbourhood. On the trunk of the apple tree just a meter away feeding off insects was the Lessor Spotted Woodpecker, an even more infrequent visitor! To have one of these magnificent birds in the garden would be amazing enough, but both at the same time? The odds on this must be pretty high. After several minutes of 'bins' sharing and camera zooming, the two birds flew off together towards the woods, as if to say *'nothing to see...bye for now'*

Diana sighed and closed the Velux. *'Why did it take you so long to get up here? You could have missed this, two of our favourite birds'* she flustered.

'Um...er...well...I just had to deal with something, sweetness and light', I smiled, like a guilty child with a water pistol behind their back.

'Is *that your work phone in your hand?'*, Diana crossed her arms and titled her head, grinning like a Siberian tiger. *'Didn't take long did it? It's not even 9.30 yet',* she said, now both eye-brows were raised.

'I think I have been caught red-handed', I will put it back in the sock drawer.*',* I replied in my very best keep calm and carry-on voice.

Just twenty days of my annual leave to go. Chances are, I would stay at the bottom of the family pecking order. I was now banking on Mo to really *foul* things up while we were away so I could at least move off the bottom of the pile.

22nd July: *From Russia without Love*

Vladimir: Please, come in Alexander. You have read the report?

Alexander: I have Mr President. It is what we expected.

Vladimir: So, they could not find evidence of Russian interference in their politics then?

Alexander: Nothing. All hearsay and speculation. It is what they *believe* could have happened which is why they are... how do the British say it...getting their knickers in a twist.

Vladimir: I have always liked your sense of humour Alexander. You seem to know which buttons to press.

Alexander: And I have always appreciated your support Mr President. One of my jobs is to keep you from pressing any buttons of course! We know we cannot beat the West with rockets so we....

Vladimir: slowly get them to tear themselves apart with stealth and subterfuge...you have told me this a million times Alexandra. It is a game of smoke and mirrors my friend. Your methods create doubt, and you leave no trace of what we *might* have done.

Alexander: Apart from *Salisbury*.

Vladmir: Not our finest hour comrade. But today, we have accomplished our goal. The British Government are fighting for their credibility after this report. Vilified for not investigating us, whether we interfered with their Brexit Referendum or not.

Alexander   They believe of course that we meddled in the 2014 Scotland Independence referendum...

Vladmir: Do not forget the 2016 US elections campaign. That was email disinformation at its best!

Alexander: And today, we are being accused by the West of firing hostile weapons as part of our space satellite programme. It is making them look paranoid as hoped for.

Vladmir: It all adds up comrade. The Russian people see the US losing grip of the pandemic, and Europe turning in on themselves. This deflects attention from our own Covid figures.

Alexander: Did you read Mr President, this week the British papers have used 'Londongrad' in their headlines? A reference to our hold on major business interests and real estate in the capital.

Vladmir: And do the authorities still believe Abramovich's *Chelski* is the hub of our business interests in London Alexander?

Alexander: It matters not what they think...they will not find any connections back to the Kremlin nor the FSB. Like, all things here, it is what they *perceive* which is far more powerful.

Vladmir: Amuse me Alexander. Where are you planning to spread your red mist next?

Alexander: We have already started aligning our message in the UK: Operation 'Winter of Discontent'

Vladmir: Aaahh the 1970s, I miss the cut and thrust of the Cold War. Is the basis of this campaign the threat of a No Deal Brexit?

Alexander: Naturally, Mr President. Combined with a flu epidemic, the threat of flooding, and a second wave of Covid-19. The messages of ill preparation and incompetence in leadership will trickle across social media. Boris has already latched onto this and the press have dubbed it the *quadruple winter whammy!*

Vladmir: The British humour eh? Keep me updated Alexander. Vodka, comrade?

Alexander: Thank you Mr President.

24th July: *The Great British Cover Up*

After months of wrangling and some would say dithering, the government has made a decision on face masks. From today in England (the Scots have had this in place already for two weeks), wearing a face covering in enclosed public spaces is compulsory. This includes shops, supermarkets, banks and post offices. The rule extends to train and bus stations and airports. Those who do not adhere to this could be fined up to £100, and will be enforced by the police, not shop workers. For practical reasons, face coverings do not have to be worn in restaurants, pubs, and gyms - or at any time when food or medication needs to be consumed. They are now optional in hairdressers, beauty salons, theatres, cinemas, opticians, and dentists. Those exempt from wearing a face covering include children under 11, people unable to do so due to physical or mental illness, and if anyone is assisting others through lip reading.

Whereas before, the scientific evidence for the wearing of face masks was not conclusively significant, Boris has now moved on new advice from SAGE and WHO recommendations. Some countries have we know been wearing face masks for many weeks now, but the key phrase used here by our political leaders is *emerging evidence* of airborne transmission of the virus. Donald Trump has also used his 'Presidential right' to carry out a U-turn on this issue, being seen in public with a mask in recent photo opportunities. Leaving the Trump administration to one side for a moment, as it only has until November in power according to our key sources in California, the question of how effective the leadership has been since the start of the pandemic is now thrown at the feet of the Johnson government.

Hindsight is a wonderful thing, but chief BBC inquisitor Laura Kuenssberg posed the question, 'what lessons have been learnt?' directly to Boris in the Downing Street garden. The prime minister was soon in defensive mode, pushing back at the Political Editor for trying to run an inquiry on the past. Boris wants to focus firmly on the months ahead. Here is an extract from the interview.

Boris: There will be plenty of opportunities to learn the lessons of what happened. You keep talking about this as though it's in the past.....we need to make sure that we're prepared for the future.

Laura: Prime Minister, isn't that precisely why this is the time to be honest about what went wrong?....This is because people need to be confident the same things do not happen again. Do you regret now that lockdown happened when it did?

Boris: I think if you listen to the scientists, the questions you have just asked are actually very open questions as they are concerned.

Laura: You said that we didn't need to ban public gatherings and then you did, the Government said we didn't need to wear face masks and now we do. You didn't pursue community testing and now it is vital, isn't this a story of delay?

Boris: If you look at the timing of every single piece of advice we got from our advisors from SAGE, you will find whenever we were told to take a particular step, actually we stuck to that advice.

Laura: Maybe your scientists were wrong?

Boris: Well Laura maybe, there were things we could have done differently. Of course there will be time to understand what exactly we could have done differently..........Covid-19 was something that was new and that we didn't understand in the way we would have liked in the first weeks and months. The single thing that we didn't see at the beginning was the extent at which it was being transmitted asymptotically.

The headline in the Daily Express after the interview read: 'Boris takes stunning swipe at his OWN advisors as he throws SAGE under the bus in grilling'. Poor Boris, you suspect Vladmir would not be subjected to such a public inquisition. That is the beauty of living in our democracy and the subsequent freedom of speech which our press and media enjoys.

26th July: *Bread*

I have, like so many others during this pandemic period, done things for the very first time. Taking advantage of the extra time and mental space during lockdown, I have started playing the ukulele (slowly), planting my own vegetables (with Diana's supervision), and writing this blog (with much needed divine support). Last week Diana made chapatis at home for the first time since her dad passed in 2011, and to help her through this emotional moment, I offered to help. Chapatis, popular as a side dish with a British curry, are unleavened flatbread originating from the Indian subcontinent and a staple food in India, Nepal, Bangladesh, Pakistan, Sri Lanka, East Africa and the Caribbean.

Diana's parents were originally from Goa, on the southwestern coastline of India, her late father a renowned cook of traditional Goanese recipes. The initial process for making chapatis is quite straight forward. Two cups of flour, one cup of water, and a pinch of salt are bound together, and then split into small balls. The trickier bit is to roll these into flat 'pancake' form, not too thick and not too thin. Once satisfied, each can be placed onto a hot chapati pan and a small amount of gee is added. Pressing down firmly with a metal spatula, the pan heat produces air bubbles under the dough to create the familiar darker charcoaled crispy surface. The result after several attempts was a set of a dozen chapatis, not all perfectly shaped, but perfectly edible.

You may have heard the expression *you are what you eat*. In this morning's online service, assistant pastor Emily took this a step further. She asked the question, *if you were bread, what type of bread would you be?* There was an online quiz site for people to refer to, but the Zoom chat box was soon full of responses such as *sourdough, multi-grain and traditional English Cob*. The justification for such choices were flimsy to say the least; the answer given from the online quiz version made little sense either. *One of the questions was 'how do you like your toast?'*. Another question was, *'which American city would you prefer to visit?'* Obviously, some dubious research design here, and I was not going to bother. Yet while Emily moved onto the Bible passage, I clicked through the questions. To my surprise, the answer came back *Rye Bread - 'You're unique!'* Unremarkable you may think, and slightly disturbing to link bread to one's character, but this outcome was rather relevant, and a little spooky.

Diana and I had tuned into this week's service from our little holiday cottage that we had booked in January. And where was this you may ask? Well, for seven days we are staying just outside the picturesque Sussex town of Rye. A favourite place of ours, a welcome change of scenery, and a dog walking paradise for Jess. Told you it was a bit *spooky*. Or perhaps a deeper meaning would become clearer? So, my ears were in full active mode as Emily continued to minister from her living room forty miles north of our current location. The scripture reading from John's Gospel Chapter 6 picks up the story of Jesus shortly after he has fed the five thousand with loaves and fishes. Despite this miracle, the people still crave more from Jesus, demanding more signs and wonders to test the authenticity of His claims to divinity.

So they asked him, *"What sign then will you give that we may see it and believe you? What will you do? Our ancestors ate the manna in the wilderness; as it is written: 'He gave them bread from heaven to eat.' "* Jesus said to them, *"Very truly I tell you, it is not Moses who has given you the bread from heaven, but it is my Father who gives you the true bread from heaven. For the bread of God is the bread that comes down from heaven and gives life to the world." "Sir,"* they said, *"always give us this bread."* Then Jesus declared, *"I am the bread of life. Whoever comes to me will never go hungry, and whoever believes in me will never be thirsty.*

This answer definitely did not come up in the online bread quiz! Jesus' response here is fundamental to who He is, and what He can do in our lives. Bread has been the staple diet for both the Ancient and Modern world, and continues to be part of our everyday lives, nourishing and sustaining us in its many forms. Yet, however much we consume, we are never completely full. What we need is the *Bread of Life*, and that comes from the never-ending power and love of Christ, who is always with us, and will never forsake us. *Emily took this message further*. To be eaten, bread needs to be broken. Only then does its full nourishment come through. If you have ever broken freshly baked bread in your hands you will know how the texture and warming odour fills the nostrils with such satisfaction!

As the Bread of Life, Jesus knew He too had to be broken for us on the cross, and in doing so released the power and authority of his life-giving blood. It is at the cross where Jesus poured out His great love for humanity, and it was in His resurrection that He became the living embodiment of God's desire to have a full relationship with us. We must not forget however that the broken body of Jesus and the full nourishment which comes from His resurrection must be a *shared* experience. In fact, as Christians we do this every time we take Holy Communion, sharing the bread with one another. The challenge is to share this Bread of Life with others in our home, at work, and with our wider friends and family.

I am still unsure how being in Rye this week is part of God's plan to share the Living Bread of Jesus. That is the beauty of God's presence in our lives. He is who He is, irrespective of our human lack of imagination. I await in anticipation.

26th July: *Leava La Espana*

We all know the problem holidaying in Britain. No, not the over-inflated accommodation prices. Er, no I was not going to mention the dubious customer service. What do you mean, the traffic jams and polluted countryside? I was referring to the Great British Summer weather! Surely, this is the blight of every staycation holiday? The rolling green hills, the picturesque harbours, the quintessential villages, the outdoor wildlife parks and the exciting theme parks - all washed up in a day's deluge. I imagine sitting in the car with the kids watching the rain lash the windows, the only source of entertainment a game of eye-spy? Perhaps I am just reflecting on my own childhood here. Is there nothing as depressing as a week of rain in Clacton?

Nowadays, if the weather outside is as grey as Yorkshire stone walls, then the kids just plug themselves in and shut out the world. Seriously though, if we could rely on the weather from May to August a little more then why go anywhere else? If you asked most people why they fly off to Tenerife, Kos or Sardinia each Summer, they will say the weather. It is the great missing ingredient for our domestic tourism industry.

Over the weekend, a quite remarkable turn of events has put paid to the holiday dreams of thousands of Brits hoping to enjoy their time in the Mediterranean Sun. The Conservative Government has suddenly decreed Spain, including the Canaries and the Balearics, as a coronavirus hot spot and placed a quarantine of two weeks on anyone returning to the UK after visiting this part of Iberia. It came as a complete shock to those already in Spain, those booked to go there, and the outbound tourist sector who have a logistical nightmare on their hands. Flights have been wiped out, bookings cancelled, and those returning with a tan now compelled to isolate for two weeks. Understandably emotions are running high with many disappointed faces and angry employees forced to take unpaid leave.

The most vehement voice of disapproval has come from the Spanish government who rely on a huge influx of British tourists to boost their own inbound industry which has already greatly suffered due to the pandemic. In an interview with the Telecino TV network, Prime Minister Sanchez called the decision as 'unjust' and totally illogical as most of Spain has lower cases than the UK. In particular, the island destinations like Mallorca have had very few reported cases at all. However, his call for the British authorities to reconsider have fallen on deaf ears as Boris Johnson warns there are signs of a 'second wave' of Covid-19 in Spain, and possibly other European destinations too. In Catalonia and Aragon, the numbers do justify a hard-line approach with the rate of infection pushing the overall cases per 100,000 in Spain to 35. This compares to the current UK rate of 14.7.

If more European and long-haul destinations get chopped from the 'travel corridor' then there could be a silver lining on the horizon for the UK domestic tourism industry. In fact, the First Minister of Scotland, Nicola Sturgeon, has said she would not book a foreign holiday at the moment due to the uncertainty, and would choose to stay in Scotland instead. The British 'Staycation' could receive a huge boost in the next couple of years, with many who usually chase the sun choosing to opt for Alton Towers, the National Parks, our unique seaside resorts and country cottages instead. This would be welcomed by the tens of thousands of workers in the leisure and hospitality industries whose jobs are under threat. The Costa Del Sol's loss could be the English Riviera's gain.

Because of health issues in recent years, Diana and myself have little urge to fly anywhere soon in the age of coronavirus, and we have often talked about finding somewhere in the UK as a weekend getaway. A place for friends and family too; a sanctuary for those who may not always have the opportunity or funds to enjoy a much needed break. Covid-19 has highlighted the importance of mental health, and maybe an opportunity will arrive soon to give something back to those we care about. The rain may always fall on these lands when least expected, but between the water drops the light is ever present.

28th July: *Duty of Care*

As you are aware by now Diana and me are fond of wildlife. In particular, we have enjoyed our attempts at entering the world of birdwatching. We have explored the rough coastal terrain of Norfolk in search of the marsh harrier, tracked the flight of sea eagles in Scotland, and stayed on Skomer Island off the Pembrokeshire coast surrounded by thousands of puffins. This week we had the chance to visit the Rye Harbour Nature Reserve, just two miles out from the lovely town itself. With strong onshore winds gusting in our faces we joined the many locals and other visitors on the coastal trail which took us through the Reserve wetlands. Jess bless her, power-walked like there was no tomorrow, and her first encounter with a stony beach by the harbour point ended in a whirlwind of pebbles and paws.

From one of the bird hides in the centre of the Reserve we managed to keep our social distance from other amateur *twitchers* and trained our binoculars at the various small wetland islands. Amongst the oyster catchers, gulls and ducks, two white flumps of feathers sat motionless 50 metres away. Could it be the rare white heron? This was debated for some time by those present, which included an interested Jess perched up on a bench looking out of the hide window. Two spoonbills possibly? A rather overweight pair of egrets perhaps? Diana, ever the twitching optimist, took a photo and claimed her heron sighting.

Jess was less impressed, keeping a beady eye on a family of ducks which was moving closer to the hide. To her credit she kept very still and not even a hint of a bark. Actually, this was one of the few times this week she *has* kept to the rules! Acting like an 18-year-old let loose on Magaluf for the first time, Jess has threatened to wreck the cottage upholstery and annoy one of our neighbours with her impression of an evil eyed guard dog.

We left the harbour oasis in awe and wonder of such a tranquil setting. It certainly cheered Diana up after she had watched *The Lost Land of the Tigers* earlier that morning in the cottage, which highlighted the plight of arguably the world's most magnificent land mammal. The programme was a repeat, filmed several years earlier, one of the presenters being the annoyingly likeable alpha male Steve Backshall. The message was simple. If humankind did not change its attitudes and behaviours towards these remarkable creatures, they would be extinct within decades. The poaching trade in China and the loss of forestation have caused their gradual decline in numbers across Asia and the Far East. Yet, there is hope. The programme showed how support from national governments, in this case Bhutan, can help to save the tiger from extinction. In fact, I looked up the latest 2020 statistics which showed tiger populations starting to recover in India, China, and Russia.

In the evening, we had our church growth group online meeting. Thankfully, the internet connection at the cottage was good, and we tuned in to see our friends. As usual we only had forty minutes on Zoom, but the eight of us had time to read through and reflect upon Psalm 8. And what a pertinent reflection it was too! The words initially focus on the Majesty of the Lord; and the writer asks why God gave humankind such an honoured place in all creation, given the awesome wonders of the entire universe.

> *When I consider your heavens,*
> *the work of your fingers,*
> *the moon and the stars,*
> *which you have set in place,*
> *what is mankind that you are mindful of them,*
> *human beings that you care for them?*

The writer of the Psalm reminds us about our duty of care for creation around us. As the dominant race, we have been assigned by God to preserve and conserve the environment, including the animals and birds which were created to share this planet Earth with us. We have been ordained to be their custodians, and this should be seen as a great honour.

You made them rulers over the works of your hands;
*   you put everything under their feet:*
all flocks and herds,
*   and the animals of the wild,*
the birds in the sky,
*   and the fish in the sea,*
all that swim the paths of the seas.
*   Lord, our Lord,*
how majestic is your name in all the earth!

By the end of the day, we were exhausted from the hot sun, the fresh sea air, and our walks through the Nature Reserve and then through nearby woodland. I looked at Jess who was fast asleep on the cool brick flooring of the cottage lounge area, and thanked God for having the opportunity of caring for her since she was eleven weeks old. Sometimes I wish I could be more of a difference to the natural world around me. More than just putting the right rubbish in the right colour bin, using rainwater to nourish our garden, and supporting the RSPB with a relatively small financial donation. Today was a timely reminder of our duty to look after the birds of the air and the beasts of the forests. With the source of the Covid-19 virus still looking to have come from human interference in nature, the onus is on *this generation* to get a lot better at being the custodians of God's creation. Mine and Diana's passion for the coastal wildlife in the UK is perhaps our place to start.

30th July: *Going Back in the Water*

Just when you thought it was safe to go back in the water. Well, *safe* to go back in public swimming pools, safe to go to beauty salons, bowling alleys, indoor performances and gatherings at sports venues that is. Just when we thought a touch of normality was returning, Boris has suddenly put the brakes on lockdown easing, throwing all our plans up and down the country into the air. A further two-week suspension has been announced following a rise in coronavirus cases.

England's chief medical officer, Prof Chris Whitty, warns the nation has 'probably reached near the limits of what can be done to reopen society'. Fears that schools may not be allowed to return in full as hoped have also been muted. Infection rates in younger people have gradually showed an increase, and if children's schooling is now a priority, other sectors of society may be used in a trade off, such as the closure of pubs and other meeting venues.

"It might come down to a question of which do you trade off against each other, and then that's a matter of prioritising. Do we think pubs are more important than schools?"
(Prof Graham Medley, Chairman of SAGE)

It is in the North of England where the spread of the disease remains the greatest cause for concern. From tomorrow, restrictions will be reintroduced for Greater Manchester, east Lancashire and parts of west Yorkshire. Essentially households are required to stay separate from each other in private and public spaces. In other parts of England, the concept of social bubbling still operates, with two *bubbles of people* allowed to meet up. Weddings had been planned on the basis these two bubbles combined meant a large gathering of family and friends, but a limit of 30 people is required, which left many desperately ringing around to say, '*sorry, please do not come, the wedding is off*'!

Better news for those like my parents who were classified as clinically vulnerable and have been shielding since lockdown started. They can now be part of groups of up to six people outdoors from 1 August; not just close family members, *and* they can form another social bubble with one other household. It is quite possible in years to come when we look back at our attempts at lockdown easing in the UK, we will be kind to ourselves and our leaders. As for now, it all seems a bit of a hotchpotch series of confusing announcements; so we all move around the dance floor, one foot forward, two steps back. Literally, we do not know whether we are coming or going.

Mask coverings have become a familiar sight now on the high street, and this afternoon in the heat of the day we visited Rye town market, with traders looking to pick up tourist business once again. Talking to the locals, coronavirus has been relatively inactive in this part of the East Sussex-Kent High Wealds region, and it is true that for many more rural towns and villages in England, the threat of contagion may seem like someone else's nightmare.

That living nightmare which is now more often than not referred to as *Covid* lingers on, and any thoughts of a return to normality any time soon are evaporating by the day. The government to its credit made it very clear at the start of lockdown easing that the chance of local restrictions and even the national reintroduction of measures to limit our freedom were highly likely. Boris and his advisors were also clear in telling everyone to use their heads and not get carried away. However, we have seen how relying on 'common sense' is unwise in a situation which is far from common.

This week a further *perfect storm* has arisen which will do little to allay the fears of decision makers. More incredibly hot weather, the common perception we are out of the woods, the problems with overseas travel, and the formal start of the Summer holiday season at home have combined to create a mad rush to the coast. In the last days of July, the major seaside resorts across all four corners of the United Kingdom were inundated with visitors. We saw these scenes before in May, but now the shackles have not only come off, but they have been discarded in place of miles of traffic jams, packed out camping and caravan sites, and wave upon wave of bodies on the beaches.

Since March 2020, we have made many personal sacrifices and as a nation kept our heads above the waterline to protect the most vulnerable around us. Despite the best Covid has thrown at us, we have held it together for the sake of the greater good. We may therefore, look back in years to come and be less kind to ourselves for our actions and behaviours in July 2020. This may be referred to as the month when we lost the gains we have worked so hard to attain. By going back in the water have we unfortunately snatched defeat from the jaws of victory?

31st July: *Inheritance*

A film came out in May this year called The Inheritance, starring Lily Collins and Simon Pegg. The plotline revolves around a familiar theme whereby an inheritance is left, monetary or otherwise, which consequently results in a series of unfortunate discoveries which threaten the unity of the family in question. If you read Agatha Christie mysteries, one of the most common motives for murder often links to family inheritance. It is not surprising, given the Bible tells us money is the root of all evil, that both in fictional stories and in real life examples, the passing down of monetary inheritance in particular can leave a sour taste with those involved. In fact, I know a number of families who no longer talk to each other as a result of squabbles caused by such a scenario.

Passing down material wealth on the account of death is one of the commonplace rituals in nearly all societies, and it seems perfectly natural to want to support the futures of the next generation. In Proverbs 13 it says,

A good person leaves an inheritance for their children's children

The Old Testament is rich in its reference to *inheritance*, and almost all of these are theological rather than legal in meaning. In the books of Deuteronomy, Numbers and Joshua for instance *to inherit* is closely aligned to the relationship between the benefactor and the recipient. Thus, God is there to freely provide material and spiritual blessings upon the Jewish people. On bequeathing the land of Canaan with all its richness to His chosen people, God starts to unfold His plan for all humankind. In the New Testament, Jesus as the Son of God uniquely qualifies Himself as His Father's heir. As such all the promises of God outlined previously sit on Jesus' shoulders, and this is why as believers in Christ, we become children of God too! We therefore by legal definition become co-heirs to God's inheritance and all the abundance of life's riches that can bring (Romans 8).

So what is this great inheritance? In short, God's inheritance to us is the possession of salvation, described in 1 Peter as the eternal and joyful existence with God Himself. This is an inheritance that can never perish, spoil, or fade, unlike the worldly treasures we seek to store up for ourselves. Nor is there the *let down bit*, say, after the will is read - this inheritance is guaranteed for all those who wish to belong to the family of God. It gets better! We do not have to wait for someone else to die (Jesus has already done this to claim God's inheritance for us). Nor do we have to wait for our own death to receive the heavenly riches. God wants us to receive His grace *now* and enjoy the riches of that grace...*now*! This could mean receiving the privilege of material wealth, but it also refers to taking on God's likeness and character, the provision of gifts of His spirit, and as noted yesterday, receiving and experiencing the wonders of creation. It is a pretty decent package! The apostle Paul puts this together in his letter to the Ephesians in a far more eloquent way than I have.

In him (Christ) we were also chosen, having been predestined according to the plan of him who works out everything in conformity with the purpose of his will, in order that we, who were the first to put our hope in Christ, might be for the praise of his glory. And you also were included in Christ when you heard the message of truth, the gospel of your salvation. When you believed, you were marked in him with a seal, the promised Holy Spirit, who is a deposit guaranteeing our inheritance until the redemption of those who are God's possession—to the praise of his glory. (Ephesians. 1 v11-14)

So what do we do if worldly treasures come our way? What if we are blessed by an inheritance gift from a friend or family member? How should we respond when there are so many that have very little? These are daily challenges to those of us who are privileged enough to not worry about where the next meal is coming from, or how the bills are to be paid. With wealth comes true responsibility, to yourself and to others. Wisdom through prayer and scripture can be sought, and faith in the One who knows best is relied upon. All week, Diana and I have looked for guidance. To our amazement the answer has been placed on our hearts with the certainty which only comes from the God who whatever our circumstance, offers the most perfect inheritance gift of all.

1st August: *The Lighthouse*

The Lighthouse shines in darkness, a lady of the lamp ensuring no-one need walk alone.

The Lighthouse guards nearby waters, with a bird's eye view of the world below.

The Lighthouse beams expectant prayer across exposed inequalities and divided loyalties.

The Lighthouse looks behind the mask, piecing jigsaws together with new identities.

The Lighthouse has a duty of care for a new normal, where audacious hope brings eternal love.

The Lighthouse stays on mission knowing perfect inheritance can be received by all.

The lighthouse fortifies the resilience of those sheltering from the raging storms.

The lighthouse feeds with the bread and wine of salvation, replenishing vital signs of life.

The lighthouse is a prayer for a world stranded in a dark web of denial.

The lighthouse is built on the battlefield frontline, our peace in a troubled sea.

Finding *The Lighthouse* was more than anything else an answer to prayer. For both of us it came like the proverbial bolt out of the blue Sussex skies. We were looking for an oasis of calm, a panacea to the months of pandemic, but also an opportunity to give sanctuary to friends and family, some who would welcome a quiet refuge from the current storm. A place to restore the spirit and convalesce the mind, even a place of retreat for those of faith, or those still seeking.

I looked back at my previous ninety-nine blog entries to discover a thread of divine hints and interventions which could only come from a higher authority. Lockdown has led to many things, but when I started my journey of writing I could not have imagined how clear the path has been laid ahead of me. For instance, if you take two earlier blog entries and put the titles together, you even have the exact location of The Lighthouse! I have been led to passages in the Bible I have never considered, and through the writing my faith has been challenged like never before.

The coronavirus pandemic has, like a huge torch from the heavens, shone upon the frailties and shortcomings of the human race. It has exposed the prejudices and inequalities in society, the limitations of scientist knowledge and politician power, and the inconsistencies of technology. In contrast, the pandemic has also brought out the best of human kindness and endeavour, the willingness to put others over self, and enhanced the ingenuity and adaptability of individuals, communities and nations. It has also opened the door for a new appreciation of nature, and a healthy perspective on the importance of looking after the mind, body, heart and soul.

Most of all I believe we will look back on the Spring and early Summer of 2020 as a crossroads in history. As the famous anecdote goes: *'Being an atheist, there is no greater authority or power than Man. He is in charge of his own destiny. We are here to decide what is right and what is wrong. If we muck things up, well....then God help us'.*

Why have we called our place of refuge on the East Sussex coast *The Lighthouse*? There is a song written by the Irish band Rend Collection which is close to mine and Diana's hearts. It has an extremely 'catchy' tune, but it is the words which have been there to encourage us in the down times and lift us above the storm clouds when needed. As we move into the next period of uncertainty in the UK, and watch on as the world struggles to contain Covid-19, these lyrics echo as a reminder of God's promise to us that His love *will* lead us through and carry us safe to shore.

In my wrestling and in my doubts
In my failures You won't walk out
Your great love will lead me through
You are the peace in my troubled sea
You are the peace in my troubled sea

In the silence, You won't let go
In the questions, Your truth will hold
Your great love will lead me through
You are the peace in my troubled sea
You are the peace in my troubled sea

My lighthouse, my lighthouse
Shining in the darkness. I will follow You
My lighthouse, my lighthouse
I will trust the promise
You will carry me safe to shore

I won't fear what tomorrow brings
With each morning I'll rise and sing
My God's love will lead me through
You are the peace in my troubled sea
You are the peace in my troubled sea

(You are my light)
My lighthouse, my lighthouse
Shining in the darkness, I will follow You
My lighthouse, my lighthouse
I will trust the promise
You will carry me safe to shore

Fire before us, You're the brightest

You will lead us through the storms
Fire before us, You're the brightest
You will lead us through the storms

My lighthouse, my lighthouse
Shining in the darkness, I will follow You
My lighthouse, my lighthouse
I will trust the promise
You will carry me safe to shore

Epilogue

At one-minute past midnight on 5th November 2020 England entered its second national lockdown. All pubs, restaurants, hospitality venues and leisure facilities closed. We have been asked to only leave home for education, work, essential item shopping, outdoor recreation and for medical reasons. When outdoors we can only mix with people from the same household or with one person from another, with a ban on mixing households indoors altogether. The lockdown has an expected timeframe of four weeks.

'Hello' then to the most unwelcomed Deja-vu. The Covid-19 second wave, as promised by scientists for months, has taken grip on the country as the late Autumn chill begins to take hold. The numbers of cases in the UK has surpassed the one million mark with an average of new cases reaching over 50,000 every day. The R rate is estimated to be at 1.5 in some parts of the UK and sadly the death toll is back in the hundreds per day. The Scientific Advisory Group for Emergencies has told the government the rate of infections and hospital admissions was now 'exceeding the reasonable worst case scenario planning levels'

We are not alone. France, Germany and Belgium this same week announced their own national lockdown restrictions. In the USA election fever has given way to the news that over 250,000 Americans have now lost their lives to coronavirus, the highest national total in the world. In the infamous words of outgoing President Donald Trump, *'stop the count'*!

The return of a lockdown has quickly focused attention on the run up to the Christmas holiday period and concerns how a restricted time of festivities would have on the nation's morale. Not wanting to be seen as a modern-day Grinch, PM Boris has vowed to rescue Christmas. The plan, according to official Government sources, is to replace this full lockdown with a tiered system more robust than the one endured to date. Populations in the North and East Midlands are already restless after bearing the brunt of Westminster's local lockdown policy. The people of Leicester have experienced heavy restrictions on their movement since March. Is it feasible to think of December 25th couped up at home in family bubbles, playing party games without embarrassing uncle George or being able to blame Grandma for the Brussel sprout smell during the Queen's speech?

"We are looking at ways to ensure that people can spend time with close family over Christmas at the end of what has been an incredibly difficult year," the PM's spokesman said this week.

As with all things Covid-19 a great balancing act is required between the needs of the health services, the state of the economy, and the physical and mental well-being of the indigenous masses. 'A window of opportunity' may be realised the spokesperson added, may be forthcoming in the form of a lessening of the tiered rules over the days around the 25th.

A small opening of hope. A shaft of light in this long tunnel. A path out of the dark woods into the clearing. The metaphors have come thick and fast. Especially as news on the results of three vaccines has been so encouraging in recent weeks. When asked when and how the great roll out would occur, the political and scientific response has been one of cautious optimism. The much maligned Health Secretary Matt Hancock has found a spring in his step as firstly the results of positive trials from the Pfizer/BioNTech vaccine hit the front pages. Found to be 90% successful in protecting people from transmission in global trials the end of the pandemic may be in sight. 'We're not there yet,' says Hancock who has probably been briefed on the huge logistical task ahead. *December ready*, has been muted, but realistically we are told, Spring will see the first stages of a mass accessible distribution through care homes, the elderly, GP surgeries and 'go-to; centres set up in venues such as sports halls.

So what of *The Lighthouse*? Our own family panacea to the pandemic. Well, for Diana, Jess and I the opportunity to find solace near the Sussex coast since the beginning of August has been nothing but a delight. We have settled in quickly to the local community way of things and made several good friends in the holiday park, mostly due to Diana's gift of freelance conversation and drop of the hat hospitality. Several of our friends in Redhill have already enjoyed the tranquillity of the lapping waves, the quietness of nature and the space and time to ponder the positive and negate the negative. Obviously, this second lockdown has meant trips to static caravan heaven have ceased. All being well we will be back in soon and inviting others to stay throughout 2021 to take advantage of this blessing bestowed upon us.

2021? What will a post-Covid world look like? Despite the inevitable hardship still to come for millions around the globe, the first lockdown period taught us to be faithful in doubt and hopeful in the face of despair. It reminded us of the fallibilities of human nature; the entrenched discrimination, the vast material inequality, and the shortcomings of those in power. As well as exposing divides in communities and nations, coronavirus also ironically shone light on the best we have to offer; the sacrificial giving to strangers, the virtue of kindness and the ingenuity of human minds.

What if the global trauma of 2020 is an *almost* unprecedented opportunity to reset humanity for the better?

Almost, because 2000 years ago God sent his son to do just that. Jesus came to Earth and live among us not only to fulfil the prophesies of the Old Testament, but through His death and resurrection He gave the whole of creation a heavenly reboot. Jesus was not just an historical figure who healed the sick and let the blind see. He was and still is the living embodiment of God's will and purpose for all of us. This one true 'Light of the World' reflected the glory of God and in doing so laid out all our sinful nature bare for all to see. But in the Kingdom of Jesus Christ we have nothing to fear. Gracefully He sees us as far more than the sum of our inequities and failings, and He believes in us far more than we can ever believe in ourselves. For His love for creation *endures forever; His faithfulness continues through all generations (*Psalm 100).

So what can a *reset humanity* look like as we gradually emerge from our time of prolonged isolation and frustration? The hope would be a 'new normal' in which we are kinder to each other, more tolerant of our differences, and more celebratory of our areas of uniqueness. Where communities thrive on open communication and loneliness is vanquished altogether. Yet, maybe overall we can finally acknowledge that human existence and the natural world are intrinsically linked as one, as God the Creator always intended them to be. Perhaps Covid-19 has made us more aware of both the power of human companionship and also the beauty of nature's rainbow in all its glorious colours. Our personal and collective responsibilities to care for each other and the environment must be the new default button, not the exception to the rule. For those of us in the comfortable privilege of relative health and wealth this surely means an even greater sense of accountability.

History though has also taught us how noble intentions become lost in the hustle and bustle. Human endeavour alone is simply not enough to bring about the change in mindset required. If we are to avoid falling back into the shadows then only the light of Christ's salvation can transform the mind, the heart and the spirit. In his letter to the Romans the apostle Paul speaks to us about the truth of Christ's transforming power;
Do not conform to the pattern of this world, but be transformed by the renewing of your mind. Then you will be able to test and approve what God's will is—his good, pleasing and perfect will. (12 v2)

Sometimes it takes a storm to clear the gutter. Sometimes it also takes time to reset. We are entering a second lockdown, and the chances are that further lockdowns will ensue in 2021 both here and around the world. Further waves will crash upon our shores, but we must keep looking at the Light and remain steadfast in our thoughts, words and deeds. As harsh as it may sound to those who have felt the full force of Covid-19, we might see this pandemic as a dark storm from which brighter futures will form. A post Covid world can be greener, fairer, more considerate, and more self-reflective. We are not *islands* standing alone against the elements, but a people who live best interconnected with each other, with the God of all creation at the core. If we humble ourselves, accept our mortality and turn our eyes to the One who is bigger than our imaginations can ever fathom, then the storms we encounter will always be quelled into submission.

Light of the world, you stepped down into darkness
Opened my eyes, let me see

Beauty that made this heart adore you
Hope of a life spent with you

Without question the year 2020 has been like no other. The pain of loss will linger way into 2021 and beyond. Revival in the human soul also takes time. Restoration and then hope in what is to come is worth fighting for. In our church services this year we have often finished by saying the following blessing to each other. Taken from the songs and liturgy of the Northumbria Community, these words are for you, me and all the families of Earth today.

> *May the peace of the Lord Christ go with you,*
> *Wherever He may send you.*
> *May He guide you through the wilderness,*
> *Protect you through the storm.*
> *May He bring you home rejoicing*
> *At the wonders He has shown you*
> *May He bring you home rejoicing once again into our doors*
> *Amen*

www.ingramcontent.com/pod-product-compliance
Lightning Source LLC
Chambersburg PA
CBHW071602080526
44588CB00010B/988